A Visual Guide to 100 High Protein Recipes for Effective Weight Loss

$$\longleftrightarrow$$

Discover Satisfying Meals Complete with Colorful Pictures and Nutritional Facts

By Ava Mitchell

Introduction

Do you want to avoid unrealistic diet plans and bland meals offering little progress? Is achieving your weight loss goal seemingly a distant dream? Unearth the solution with Ava Mitchell's "A Visual Guide to 100 High Protein Recipes for Effective Weight Loss".

This enticing guide is no ordinary recipe book. It is a carefully curated collection of 100 high-protein recipes designed to satisfy your palate while aiding your weight loss journey. This book brings the dining experience to life, allowing you to visualize your culinary masterpiece before taking the first step in its preparation.

Be prepared to be captivated by each page as you discover mouthwatering dishes that strike the perfect balance between taste and nutrition. Comprehensive nutritional facts accompany each recipe, so you're not just cooking – you understand the science behind each ingredient and its impact on your body. Mitchell's step-by-step instructions, tips, and tricks make healthy cooking an approachable endeavor, not daunting task.

Whether you're a novice in the kitchen or an accomplished home cook, this book will revolutionize how you view diet and nutrition. "A Visual Guide to 100 High Protein Recipes for Effective Weight Loss" isn't just about losing weight. It's about embarking on a journey towards a healthier lifestyle. Start this journey today, and redefine your relationship with food.

Transform your weight loss journey from a tiresome struggle into a delightful culinary adventure with Ava Mitchell's groundbreaking guide.

Table of Contents

Chapter 01: Rise and Shine Protein-Packed Breakfasts

Recipe 01: Mixed Berry, Granola and Yogurt Parfaits

Experience the power of protein-packed breakfast with these delightful Mixed berries, Granola, and Yogurt Parfaits. A balance of sweet fruits, creamy yogurt, and crunchy Granola, it's a delicious way to kickstart your day while focusing on weight loss.

Servings: 4

Prepping Time: 15 minutes

Cook Time: 0 minutes

Difficulty: Easy

Ingredients:

- ✓ 2 cups mixed berries (blueberries, strawberries, raspberries)

- ✓ 2 cups Greek yogurt
- ✓ 1 cup Granola
- ✓ 4 tbsp honey
- ✓ 1/4 cup chia seeds

Step-by-Step Preparation:

1. Layer 1/4 cup of yogurt at the bottom of each serving glass or bowl.
2. Sprinkle a layer of Granola, followed by a layer of mixed berries.
3. Drizzle honey over the berries, then sprinkle with chia seeds.
4. Repeat these layers until the glass or bowl is full, finishing with a dollop of yogurt and a sprinkle of Granola and berries.
5. Serve immediately or refrigerate overnight for a chilled breakfast.

Nutritional Facts: (Per serving)

- ❖ Calories: 280
- ❖ Protein: 20g
- ❖ Carbs: 35g
- ❖ Fat: 8g
- ❖ Fiber: 7g

Indulge in the refreshing and nourishing Mixed Berry, Granola, and Yogurt Parfaits without derailing your weight loss journey. This protein-rich, high-fiber breakfast will keep you satisfied and energetic throughout the morning, proving that healthy eating can be delicious and enjoyable.

Recipe 02: Egg Muffins With Kale and Ground Turkey

Begin your day with a healthy, high-protein kick! These egg muffins, brimming with kale and ground turkey, are a flavorful, nutritious breakfast option. Ideal for weight loss and super easy to prepare, they'll surely be your new morning favorite.

Servings: 12 Muffins

Prepping Time: 15 Minutes

Cook Time: 25 Minutes

Difficulty: Easy

Ingredients:

- ✓ 12 large eggs
- ✓ 1 cup ground turkey
- ✓ 2 cups kale, chopped
- ✓ 1 medium onion, diced

- ✓ 2 cloves garlic, minced
- ✓ Salt and pepper to taste
- ✓ Non-stick cooking spray

Step-by-Step Preparation:

1. Preheat your oven to 375°F (190°C). Grease a muffin tin with non-stick spray.

2. In a pan, cook ground turkey until no longer pink. Add onions, garlic, and cook until onions are translucent.

3. Add kale and cook until wilted. Season with salt and pepper.

4. Beat eggs in a large bowl. Stir in the cooked turkey and kale mixture.

5. Pour the mixture into the muffin tin, filling each about 3/4 full.

6. Bake for 20-25 minutes, until set and lightly golden.

7. Let cool for a few minutes, then remove from the tin. Serve warm.

Nutritional Facts: (Per serving)

- ❖ Calories: 140
- ❖ Protein: 12g
- ❖ Fat: 8g
- ❖ Carbohydrates: 2g
- ❖ Fiber: 0.5g
- ❖ Sugar: 0.5g

Breakfast just became your secret weapon for weight loss! These egg muffins are delicious and keep you full and satisfied. Perfect for on-the-go or meal prep, this recipe will make your mornings as healthy as they are flavorful.

Recipe 03: Avocado Toast with Egg

Immerse yourself in the world of healthy and delicious breakfasts with our Avocado Toast with Egg. Packed with proteins, healthy fats, and nutrient-dense ingredients dish is ideal for those seeking high-protein meals to support weight loss.

Servings: 2

Prepping Time: 10 minutes

Cook Time: 5 minutes

Difficulty: Easy

Ingredients:

- ✓ 2 slices of whole-grain bread
- ✓ 1 ripe avocado
- ✓ 2 large eggs
- ✓ Salt and pepper to taste
- ✓ 1 teaspoon lemon juice

- ✓ 1 tablespoon olive oil
- ✓ Chopped parsley or cilantro for garnish

Step-by-Step Preparation:

1. Toast your bread until golden and crispy.
2. In a bowl, mash the avocado and mix with lemon juice, salt, and pepper.
3. Spread the mashed avocado onto each slice of toast.
4. In a pan, cook the eggs (sunny side up or scrambled) with olive oil.
5. Place the cooked eggs on top of the avocado toast.
6. Season with additional salt and pepper and garnish with parsley or cilantro.

Nutritional Facts: (Per serving)

- ❖ Calories: 320
- ❖ Protein: 12g
- ❖ Carbs: 25g
- ❖ Fat: 20g
- ❖ Fiber: 9g
- ❖ Sugar: 3g

With our Avocado Toast with Egg, starting your day on a nutritious and high-protein note becomes a delightful experience. Easy to prepare and incredibly satisfying, this breakfast recipe is a foolproof way to support your weight loss journey without compromising taste or health.

Recipe 04: Quinoa With Nuts Milk and Berries

Start your day with this nutritious Organic Breakfast Quinoa with Nuts, Milk, and Berries. It's a high-protein meal designed to support your weight loss goals, combining sweet berries, creamy nut milk, and the wholesome goodness of quinoa.

Servings: 2

Prepping Time: 10 minutes

Cook Time: 15 minutes

Difficulty: Easy

Ingredients:

- ✓ 1 cup of organic quinoa
- ✓ 2 cups of nut milk
- ✓ 1 cup of mixed berries (raspberries, blueberries, and strawberries)
- ✓ 2 tablespoons of honey
- ✓ 1/4 cup of mixed nuts (almonds, walnuts, and cashews)

✓ A pinch of salt

Step-by-Step Preparation:

1. Rinse the quinoa under cold water and drain.

2. Bring the nut milk to a boil in a saucepan, and add the quinoa and a pinch of salt. Simmer for 15 minutes or until quinoa is fluffy.

3. Stir in the honey, then top with mixed berries and nuts.

4. Serve immediately and enjoy your high-protein breakfast.

Nutritional Facts: (Per serving)

❖ Calories: 350

❖ Protein: 12g

❖ Carbohydrates: 55g

❖ Fat: 10g

❖ Fiber: 6g

End your morning hunger with this delightful Organic Breakfast Quinoa. It's packed with protein and flavors to satisfy you, aiding your weight loss journey. Easy to prepare, this dish is not just a meal but a colorful, tasty way to start your day.

Recipe 05: Cranberry Sauce and Pudding Of Chia Seeds

Indulge in a festive breakfast that pairs tangy cranberry sauce with a wholesome chia seed pudding, all beautifully garnished with homemade ginger star-shaped biscuits. This high-protein, low-calorie meal is the perfect start to your day, aiding your weight loss journey while celebrating the season's joy.

Servings: 4

Prepping Time: 20 minutes

Cook Time: 2 hours (for the chia pudding to set)

Difficulty: Easy

Ingredients:

- ✓ 1/2 cup Chia Seeds
- ✓ 2 cups Almond Milk
- ✓ 2 tablespoons Honey
- ✓ 1 cup Fresh Cranberries

- ✓ 1/4 cup Sugar
- ✓ 1/4 cup Water
- ✓ 1/2 cup Whole Wheat Flour
- ✓ 1 teaspoon Ground Ginger
- ✓ 1/4 teaspoon Baking Powder

Step-by-Step Preparation:

1. Mix chia seeds, almond milk, and honey in a bowl. Stir well and refrigerate for at least 2 hours.

2. In a saucepan, combine cranberries, sugar, and water. Simmer until cranberries burst and the sauce thickens. Cool.

3. Preheat oven to 350°F. Mix flour, ginger, and baking powder. Roll out and cut into star shapes. Bake for 10-12 minutes.

4. Serve chia pudding with a dollop of cranberry sauce and a ginger star biscuit.

Nutritional Facts: (Per serving)

- ❖ Calories: 250
- ❖ Protein: 10g
- ❖ Carbohydrates: 32g
- ❖ Fat: 10g
- ❖ Fiber: 8g
- ❖ Sugar: 12g

Treat yourself to a morning feast that promises to satisfy your taste buds and provide you with a nutritious, protein-packed start. This cranberry and chia seed pudding, adorned with homemade ginger star biscuits, is a delightful blend of flavors and textures, making weight loss an enjoyable endeavor. A breakfast was genuinely worth waking up for!

Recipe 06: Scrambled Eggs With Smoked Salmon

Kickstart your day with this high-protein, low-calorie breakfast dish that will keep you satisfied while helping you manage your weight. It combines deliciously fluffy scrambled eggs with delectable smoked salmon, served atop a slice of hearty sourdough toast.

Servings: 2

Prepping Time: 5 minutes

Cook Time: 10 minutes

Difficulty: Easy

Ingredients:

- ✓ 4 large eggs

- ✓ 100g smoked salmon

- ✓ 2 slices of sourdough bread

- ✓ 1 tablespoon of olive oil

- ✓ Salt and pepper to taste
- ✓ Chopped fresh chives for garnish

Step-by-Step Preparation:

1. Beat the eggs in a bowl, adding salt and pepper to taste.

2. Heat the olive oil in a non-stick pan over medium heat.

3. Pour the beaten eggs into the pan and cook, stirring occasionally, until soft and slightly runny.

4. Toast the sourdough bread and divide the scrambled eggs between the two slices.

5. Top each with smoked salmon and garnish with chives.

Nutritional Facts: (Per serving)

- ❖ Calories: 350
- ❖ Protein: 28g
- ❖ Carbohydrates: 30g
- ❖ Fat: 14g
- ❖ Fiber: 2g
- ❖ Sugar: 2g

Start your weight loss journey the right way with this Scrambled Eggs with Smoked Salmon on Sourdough Toast recipe. It's an ideal breakfast dish that's high in protein to fuel your day and low in calories to support your weight loss efforts. Make this your go-to morning meal for a delightful culinary experience that doesn't compromise on nutrition.

Recipe 07: Matcha Overnight Oats With Kiwi And Peach Fruits, Chia Seeds

Kickstart your day with a healthy, protein-rich breakfast: Matcha Overnight Oats With Kiwi And Peach Fruits, Chia Seeds. This dish marries the earthy flavors of matcha with the sweetness of fresh fruits, all while being a delicious tool in your weight loss journey.

Servings: 2

Prepping Time: 10 minutes

Cook Time: Overnight

Difficulty: Easy

Ingredients:

- ✓ 1 cup rolled oats
- ✓ 1.5 cups almond milk
- ✓ 2 tablespoons matcha powder
- ✓ 1 tablespoon chia seeds

✓ 2 teaspoons honey or sweetener of choice

✓ 1 kiwi, diced

✓ 1 peach, diced

Step-by-Step Preparation:

1. Mix the oats, almond milk, matcha powder, chia seeds, and sweetener in a bowl.

2. Divide the mixture between two mason jars.

3. Top each jar with diced kiwi and peach.

4. Cover the jars and place them in the fridge overnight.

5. In the morning, stir well and enjoy the cold.

Nutritional Facts: (Per serving)

❖ Calories: 300

❖ Protein: 11g

❖ Carbohydrates: 50g

❖ Fat: 7g

❖ Fiber: 10g

❖ Sugar: 12g

Start your mornings with a power-packed, delicious Matcha Overnight Oats With Kiwi And Peach Fruits, Chia Seeds breakfast. Its complex carbohydrates, high fiber, and protein balance will keep you full and satisfied, helping curb those snack cravings throughout the day. Here's to healthy weight loss!

Recipe 08: Scramble Tofu With Vegetables

Kickstart your day with this high-protein, low-fat breakfast dish. Scrambled Tofu with Vegetables in a Pan is a delicious and easy way to fuel your weight loss journey. Packed with nutrients and bursting with flavor, it will keep you satisfied until lunchtime.

Servings: 2

Prepping Time: 10 minutes

Cook Time: 15 minutes

Difficulty: Easy

Ingredients:

- ✓ 200g firm tofu, crumbled
- ✓ 1 cup assorted vegetables (like bell peppers, spinach, and mushrooms), chopped
- ✓ 1 small onion, chopped
- ✓ 2 garlic cloves, minced
- ✓ 1 tbsp olive oil

- ✓ 2 tsp soy sauce

- ✓ Salt and pepper to taste

- ✓ Fresh herbs for garnish

Step-by-Step Preparation:

1. Heat the olive oil in a pan over medium heat.

2. Add the onion and garlic and sauté until translucent.

3. Add the assorted vegetables and cook until tender.

4. Add the crumbled tofu, soy sauce, salt, and pepper. Stir well to combine.

5. Cook for another 5 minutes, until tofu is golden.

6. Garnish with fresh herbs and serve hot.

Nutritional Facts: (Per serving)

- ❖ Calories: 220

- ❖ Protein: 18g

- ❖ Carbs: 10g

- ❖ Fat: 12g

- ❖ Fiber: 4g

Enjoy the health benefits and the delicious taste of this Scrambled Tofu with Vegetables in a Pan. Whether you're aiming for weight loss or simply a healthier lifestyle, this protein-rich breakfast is the perfect start to your day! It's easy, nutritious, and undeniably satisfying.

Recipe 09: Fried Cottage Cheese Pancakes

Start your day right with these nutritious fried cottage cheese pancakes, a high-protein meal for weight loss, beautifully complemented with berry jam, almonds, and mint. A healthful blend of flavors that not only excite your taste buds but also contributes to your weight loss journey.

Servings: 2

Prepping Time: 15 minutes

Cook Time: 10 minutes

Difficulty: Easy

Ingredients:

- ✓ 1 cup cottage cheese
- ✓ 1/4 cup almond flour
- ✓ 2 large eggs
- ✓ 1 tablespoon honey
- ✓ Pinch of salt

- ✓ 2 tablespoons coconut oil (for frying)
- ✓ 1/2 cup berry jam
- ✓ 1/4 cup almonds, slivered
- ✓ Fresh mint leaves

Step-by-Step Preparation:

1. Combine cottage cheese, almond flour, eggs, honey, and salt in a bowl until smooth.
2. Heat the coconut oil in a non-stick pan over medium heat.
3. Spoon the batter onto the pan and flatten it with a spatula. Cook until golden brown on both sides.
4. Serve the pancakes with a dollop of berry jam, a sprinkle of slivered almonds, and fresh mint leaves on top.

Nutritional Facts: (Per serving)

- ❖ Calories: 320 kcal
- ❖ Protein: 18g
- ❖ Carbohydrates: 22g
- ❖ Fat: 16g
- ❖ Fiber: 3g
- ❖ Sugar: 12g

Start your mornings with these delightful and nutritious cottage cheese pancakes. The high protein content will keep you satisfied for longer, aiding in weight management. The almonds provide a good crunch, while the berry jam brings a tangy sweetness that perfectly complements the soft, creamy pancakes. Indeed a breakfast worth waking up for!

Recipe 10: Classic Banana Nut Muffins

Kickstart your weight-loss journey with these delicious and filling Classic Banana Nut Muffins. High in protein and packed with natural sweetness, these muffins are perfect for a quick and satisfying breakfast on the go.

Servings: 12 muffins

Prepping Time: 15 minutes

Cook Time: 20 minutes

Difficulty: Easy

Ingredients:

- ✓ 3 ripe bananas
- ✓ 1/3 cup unsweetened almond milk
- ✓ 2 eggs
- ✓ 1 cup almond flour
- ✓ 1/2 cup protein powder
- ✓ 1/4 cup honey

- ✓ 1 teaspoon baking soda
- ✓ 1/2 teaspoon cinnamon
- ✓ 1/2 cup chopped walnuts

Step-by-Step Preparation:

1. Preheat the oven to 350°F and line a muffin tin with liners.

2. Mash the bananas in a bowl. Add almond milk, eggs, and honey, mixing until well combined.

3. Combine almond flour, protein powder, baking soda, and cinnamon in another bowl. Gradually add this to the banana mixture, stirring until just mixed.

4. Fold in the chopped walnuts and divide the batter among the muffin cups.

5. Bake for 20 minutes or until a toothpick inserted in the center comes clean.

Nutritional Facts: (Per serving)

- ❖ Calories: 160
- ❖ Protein: 7g
- ❖ Fat: 9g
- ❖ Carbs: 12g
- ❖ Fiber: 3g
- ❖ Sugar: 6g

These Classic Banana Nut Muffins are a fantastic high-protein breakfast option that promotes weight loss. Enjoy the burst of energy they provide without the guilt of unwanted calories. Easy to prepare, they're perfect for busy mornings and can be stored for future breakfasts or healthy snacks throughout the week.

Chapter 02: Revitalize with Mid-Morning Protein Feasts

Recipe 11: Pancake With Fruits and Cinnamon

Welcome to your health-focused journey where taste meets nutrition! Enjoy a delicious mid-morning brunch of Gluten-Free High Protein Pancakes topped with fresh fruits and a dash of cinnamon. This guilt-free delight is perfect for those looking to lose weight without compromising the joy of eating.

Servings: 4

Prepping Time: 10 minutes

Cook Time: 20 minutes

Difficulty: Easy

Ingredients:

- ✓ 1 cup gluten-free oat flour

- ✓ 2 scoops vanilla protein powder
- ✓ 1 teaspoon baking powder
- ✓ 2 eggs and 1/2 cup almond milk
- ✓ 1 teaspoon vanilla extract
- ✓ Assorted fruits for topping (banana, berries, apple)
- ✓ 1/2 teaspoon cinnamon powder

Step-by-Step Preparation:

1. Combine oat flour, protein powder, and baking powder in a bowl.
2. In another bowl, whisk eggs, almond milk, and vanilla extract.
3. Gradually add the wet ingredients to the dry ingredients, mixing until combined.
4. Heat a non-stick pan over medium heat, ladle batter onto the pan, and cook until bubbles form on the surface, then flip and cook the other side.
5. Serve pancakes with fresh fruits and a sprinkle of cinnamon on top.

Nutritional Facts: (Per serving)

- ❖ Calories: 220 kcal
- ❖ Protein: 20 g
- ❖ Carbohydrates: 30 g
- ❖ Fat: 4 g
- ❖ Fiber: 5 g
- ❖ Sugar: 10 g

Wrap up your meal with a delectable blend of protein-rich, gluten-free goodness. This high-protein pancake recipe will meet your dietary needs and satisfy your taste buds. Indulge in this simple, quick, and delicious brunch, an ideal choice for weight loss that doesn't sacrifice flavor for health.

Recipe 12: Potato Crust Quiche With Spinach

Enjoy a delightful mid-morning treat with this delicious, high-protein Potato Crust Quiche filled with spinach, bacon, and goat cheese. Ideal for weight loss, this meal is a balance of wholesome ingredients and satiating protein, perfect for a tasty brunch or a light lunch.

Servings: 6

Prepping Time: 20 minutes

Cook Time: 45 minutes

Difficulty: Intermediate

Ingredients:

- ✓ 2 large potatoes, thinly sliced
- ✓ 200g fresh spinach
- ✓ 6 strips of bacon, cooked and crumbled
- ✓ 100g goat cheese, crumbled
- ✓ 6 large eggs

✓ 1/4 cup milk

✓ Salt and pepper to taste

Step-by-Step Preparation:

1. Preheat oven to 375°F (190°C), line a pie dish with the potato slices, and bake for 15 minutes.

2. Meanwhile, sauté spinach until wilted and set aside.

3. In a bowl, whisk eggs, milk, salt, and pepper.

4. Layer the spinach, bacon, and goat cheese on the pre-baked potato crust.

5. Pour the egg mixture over the layered ingredients.

6. Bake for 30 minutes or until set. Let cool before serving.

Nutritional Facts: (Per serving)

❖ Calories: 280

❖ Protein: 20g

❖ Carbs: 15g

❖ Fat: 15g

❖ Fiber: 2g

Reward your weight loss journey with this tasty, nutrient-packed Potato Crust Quiche. Whether as a satisfying brunch or a protein-filled lunch, this dish will keep you feeling full, aiding your fitness journey while tantalizing your tastebuds with its heavenly blend of ingredients.

Recipe 13: Chickpea Omelette Made with Garbanzo Bean Flour

Kickstart your day with this vibrant and delicious Chickpea Omelette made with chickpea flour and topped with fresh tomato and red bell pepper. It's a perfect high-protein, weight-loss-friendly brunch with a zesty arugula salad and refreshing lemon wedges.

Servings: 2

Prepping Time: 15 minutes

Cook Time: 10 minutes

Difficulty: Easy

Ingredients:

- ✓ 1 cup chickpea flour
- ✓ 1.5 cups water
- ✓ 1 tomato, chopped
- ✓ 1 red bell pepper, chopped

- ✓ 2 cups arugula
- ✓ 2 lemon wedges
- ✓ Salt and pepper to taste
- ✓ Olive oil for cooking

Step-by-Step Preparation:

1. Mix chickpea flour with water, salt, and pepper in a bowl. Whisk until smooth.

2. Heat oil in a pan, pour half the batter and cook for 2-3 minutes.

3. Add half the tomato and bell pepper, then flip and cook for 2-3 minutes. Repeat for the second omelet.

4. Serve the omelets hot with arugula salad and lemon wedges on the side.

Nutritional Facts: (Per serving)

- ❖ Calories: 250 kcal
- ❖ Protein: 14g
- ❖ Fat: 5g
- ❖ Carbohydrates: 40g
- ❖ Fiber: 10g
- ❖ Sugars: 8g

Savor this chickpea omelet and enjoy the fusion of taste, nutrition, and satisfaction. Ideal for those mornings when you're craving a heartier breakfast, it promises to keep you full while helping you on your weight-loss journey. Simple, delicious, and quick to prepare - it's the perfect brunch recipe for your healthier lifestyle.

Recipe 14: Greek Yoghurt With Honey and Walnuts

This Greek Yoghurt with Honey and Walnuts dish is a refreshing high-protein meal perfect for weight loss. A traditional blend of creamy, tangy, and sweet flavors, it's an ideal choice for a mid-morning snack or a wholesome brunch.

Servings: 2

Prepping Time: 5 minutes

Cook Time: No cooking required

Difficulty: Easy

Ingredients:

- ✓ 2 cups of Greek yogurt

- ✓ 4 tablespoons of honey

- ✓ 1/2 cup of walnuts, chopped

- ✓ Fresh mint leaves for garnish (optional)

Step-by-Step Preparation:

1. Spoon Greek yogurt into two bowls.

2. Drizzle each serving with 2 tablespoons of honey.

3. Sprinkle chopped walnuts evenly over the yogurt.

4. Garnish with fresh mint leaves if desired.

Nutritional Facts: (Per serving)

❖ Calories: 370

❖ Protein: 20g

❖ Carbs: 30g

❖ Fat: 20g

❖ Fiber: 2g

Enjoy a touch of Greek tradition with this quick, nutritious meal. Greek Yoghurt with Honey and Walnuts are high in protein and a fantastic source of healthy fats, supporting your weight loss journey while deliciously satiating your cravings.

Recipe 15: Blueberry Muffins

Kickstart your morning or refuel midday with these delightful Blueberry Muffins with an Oat Crumble. High in protein, these little gems are perfect for those on a weight loss journey, offering a balanced, flavorful option for brunch or a snack.

Servings: 12 muffins

Prepping Time: 15 minutes

Cook Time: 25 minutes

Difficulty: Easy

Ingredients:

- ✓ 2 cups whole wheat flour and 1 cup blueberries
- ✓ 1 cup unsweetened almond milk and 2 large eggs
- ✓ 3/4 cup natural sweetener (like Stevia) and 1/2 cup Greek yogurt
- ✓ 1/4 cup rolled oats and 2 tbsp honey
- ✓ 1 tsp baking powder

✓ 1/2 tsp baking soda and Pinch of salt

Step-by-Step Preparation:

1. Preheat your oven to 350°F (175°C) and line a muffin tin with paper liners.

2. Combine the flour, sweetener, baking powder, baking soda, and salt in a large bowl.

3. Whisk together the eggs, Greek yogurt, and almond milk in another bowl.

4. Slowly add the wet ingredients to the dry, mixing until combined.

5. Fold in the blueberries.

6. Spoon the mixture into the muffin tin, filling each to about 2/3 full.

7. Mix the oats and honey in a small bowl to create the crumble and sprinkle over the muffins.

8. Bake for 25 minutes or until a toothpick comes out clean.

Nutritional Facts: (Per serving)

❖ Calories: 150

❖ Protein: 8g

❖ Carbohydrates: 22g

❖ Fat: 4g

❖ Fiber: 3g

❖ Sugar: 8g

Concluding your culinary adventure, you'll be delighted with the delicious and nutritious result. These high-protein Blueberry Muffins with an Oat Crumble provide the perfect balance of sweetness and wholesome nutrition and complement your weight loss efforts. Enjoy them with a cup of green tea or your favorite beverage for an ideal brunch or mid-morning snack.

Recipe 16: Wok Stir Fried Tofu and Vegetables

The Wok stir-fried tofu and vegetables with satay sauce are an excellent choice for weight loss and a protein-rich treat. This vibrant and flavorful dish marries wholesome tofu and fresh vegetables with a delightful, tangy satay sauce, creating a healthy and delicious brunch or mid-morning meal.

Servings: 4

Prepping Time: 15 Minutes

Cook Time: 20 Minutes

Difficulty: Easy

Ingredients:

- ✓ 1 block of firm tofu
- ✓ 1 cup of assorted vegetables (bell peppers, broccoli, and carrots)
- ✓ 2 tablespoons of olive oil
- ✓ 1/2 cup of satay sauce
- ✓ Salt and pepper to taste

Step-by-Step Preparation:

1. Press and cube the tofu, and set aside.

2. Chop the vegetables into bite-sized pieces.

3. Heat the oil in a wok over medium-high heat.

4. Add tofu and vegetables, stir-frying until they're tender and the tofu is golden brown.

5. Add satay sauce and stir until everything is evenly coated.

6. Season with salt and pepper, and serve warm.

Nutritional Facts: (Per serving)

* ❖ Calories: 240

* ❖ Protein: 18g

* ❖ Fat: 12g

* ❖ Carbohydrates: 18g

* ❖ Dietary fiber: 4g

Here is your healthy, protein-rich wok stir-fried tofu and vegetables with satay sauce. This easy-to-prepare dish, packed with nutrients and flavor, is the perfect addition to your weight loss menu. Enjoy the refreshing crunch of stir-fried vegetables, the satisfying bite of tofu, and the savory kick of satay sauce. Stay healthy and relish every bite!

Recipe 17: Egg Wrap With Turkey and Cheese

Packed with protein and bursting with flavor, our Egg Wrap with Turkey and Cheese makes the perfect mid-morning or brunch dish. Easy to prepare and loaded with nutritious ingredients, this recipe aids in weight loss and gives you the energy to power through your day.

Servings: 2

Prepping Time: 10 minutes

Cook Time: 15 minutes

Difficulty: Easy

Ingredients:

- ✓ 4 large eggs
- ✓ 4 slices of turkey
- ✓ 2 slices of low-fat cheese
- ✓ 2 tablespoons of olive oil
- ✓ Salt and pepper to taste

✓ 1/2 cup of fresh spinach (optional)

Step-by-Step Preparation:

1. Whisk the eggs, salt, and pepper in a bowl.

2. Heat 1 tablespoon of olive oil in a non-stick pan.

3. Pour the whisked eggs into the pan, ensuring an even layer.

4. Add turkey and cheese slices to one-half of the egg wrap and let it cook until the cheese melts.

5. Fold the egg wrap in half, cook for another minute, and serve with fresh spinach if desired.

Nutritional Facts: (Per serving)

❖ Calories: 300

❖ Protein: 25g

❖ Carbs: 3g

❖ Fat: 21g

❖ Fiber: 1g

Wrap up your morning hunger with this Egg Wrap with Turkey and Cheese. A high-protein meal that satiates your appetite while aiding in weight loss. This easy-to-make, nutritious dish is perfect for those seeking a balance of taste and health in their morning or brunch routine.

Recipe 18: Healthy Brunch Power Bowl

Revitalize your mid-morning routine with our Healthy Brunch Power Bowl. Packed with the goodness of natural yogurt, chia seeds, fruits, and vegetables easy-to-make recipe is a perfect high-protein meal to aid your weight loss journey.

Servings: 2

Prepping Time: 10 minutes

Cook Time: 0 minutes (No cooking required)

Difficulty: Easy

Ingredients:

- ✓ 2 cups of natural yogurt
- ✓ 2 tablespoons of Chia seeds
- ✓ 1 banana
- ✓ 1 kiwi
- ✓ 2 stalks of celery

✓   2 cups of spinach

Step-by-Step Preparation:

1. Slice the banana and kiwi into thin pieces.

2. Chop the celery stalks finely.

3. In a bowl, layer spinach, celery, sliced fruits, and chia seeds on top of the yogurt.

4. Mix gently before serving.

Nutritional Facts: (Per serving)

❖ Calories: 250

❖ Protein: 12g

❖ Carbs: 30g

❖ Fiber: 7g

❖ Fat: 8g

Relish this Healthy Brunch Power Bowl, a delicious way to nourish your body and support your weight loss goals. Its flavors will leave you satiated till lunch, powering your morning with the best of nature's bounty.

Recipe 19: Egg Muffins With Ham, Cheese and Vegetables

Kick-start your day with these Protein Packed Oatmeal Pancakes. This wholesome recipe combines simple ingredients, bursting with the goodness of oats and proteins, ensuring you're fully charged and ready to take on the world.

Servings: 4

Prepping Time: 10 Minutes

Cook Time: 15 Minutes

Difficulty: Easy

Ingredients:

- ✓ 2 cups rolled oats
- ✓ 1 1/4 cups milk
- ✓ 1 ripe banana
- ✓ 2 eggs

- ✓ 1 scoop of your favorite protein powder
- ✓ 1 teaspoon vanilla extract
- ✓ 1/2 teaspoon cinnamon
- ✓ 2 teaspoons baking powder
- ✓ 1/4 teaspoon salt

Step-by-Step Preparation:

1. Blend all ingredients in a blender until smooth.
2. Heat a non-stick pan on medium heat.
3. Pour 1/4 cup of the batter onto the pan.
4. Cook each side for about 2-3 minutes until golden brown.
5. Repeat with the remaining batter.

Nutritional Facts: (Per serving)

- ❖ Calories: 350
- ❖ Protein: 18g
- ❖ Fat: 6g
- ❖ Carbohydrates: 55g
- ❖ Fiber: 8g
- ❖ Sugar: 10g

Enjoy the feeling of nourishment and satisfaction after indulging in these delicious pancakes. Not only are they packed with protein, but they are also heart-healthy and will keep you satiated until lunchtime. This is breakfast done right, so treat yourself!

Recipe 20: Home Made Healthy Brunch

Start your day with a nutritious, power-packed brunch with this Homemade Healthy Brunch Super Food. Bursting with granola, yogurt, fruits, nuts, chia seeds, pollen grain, and acai berry powder perfect mid-morning meal to aid your weight loss journey.

Servings: 2

Prepping Time: 15 minutes

Cook Time: 0 minutes

Difficulty: Easy

Ingredients:

- ✓ 1 cup granola
- ✓ 1 cup Greek yogurt
- ✓ 1 cup assorted fresh fruits
- ✓ 2 tablespoons nuts
- ✓ 1 tablespoon chia seeds

- ✓ 1 tablespoon pollen grain
- ✓ 1 tablespoon acai berry powder

Step-by-Step Preparation:

1. Begin by layering half the Greek yogurt at the bottom of a bowl.

2. Add a layer of granola, followed by half the fresh fruits.

3. Sprinkle with half the chia seeds, nuts, and pollen grains.

4. Repeat the layers.

5. Top with acai berry powder and serve.

Nutritional Facts: (Per serving)

- ❖ Calories: 350

- ❖ Protein: 14g

- ❖ Fat: 10g

- ❖ Carbohydrates: 50g

- ❖ Dietary fiber: 8g

Delight in this wholesome Homemade Healthy Brunch Super Food for a genuinely satisfying start to your day. With high protein and rich fiber content, this brunch dish is a must-try for weight loss patients. So, why wait? Whip this vibrant, crunchy, and creamy treat for your next brunch!

Chapter 03: Lean and Mean High-Protein Lunches

Recipe 21: Buddha Bowl Lunch With Grilled Chicken

Discover the art of mindful eating with this nourishing Buddha Bowl lunch. Packed with protein-rich grilled chicken, quinoa, and a vibrant medley of veggies, a delicious, satiating dish to support your weight loss journey.

Servings: 4

Prepping Time: 20 minutes

Cook Time: 15 minutes

Difficulty: Easy

Ingredients:

- ✓ 2 boneless chicken breasts

- ✓ 2 cups cooked quinoa

- ✓ 2 cups fresh spinach and 1 avocado, sliced
- ✓ 1 cup Brussels sprouts, halved
- ✓ 1 cup cherry tomatoes, halved
- ✓ 1 cucumber, sliced
- ✓ Olive oil, salt, and pepper to taste

Step-by-Step Preparation:

1. Preheat your grill to medium-high heat and cook chicken breasts until thoroughly cooked.

2. In a pan over medium heat, sauté Brussels sprouts in olive oil until tender.

3. Assemble your Buddha Bowl starting with a bed of quinoa, then neatly arrange your grilled chicken, spinach, avocado slices, sautéed Brussels sprouts, cherry tomatoes, and cucumber.

4. Season with salt, pepper, and a drizzle of olive oil.

Nutritional Facts: (Per serving)

- ❖ Calories: 450
- ❖ Protein: 35g
- ❖ Carbs: 45g
- ❖ Fat: 15g
- ❖ Fiber: 8g
- ❖ Sodium: 200mg

Say goodbye to bland lunch meals and welcome this wholesome, high-protein Buddha Bowl into your routine. With an array of nutrients from various colorful vegetables, plus lean protein and whole grains, this is the perfect meal to fuel your body while aiding in weight loss.

Recipe 22: Turkey Chili Stewed With Black and White Beans

Experience delightful flavors with this Turkey Chili stewed with black and white beans, tomatoes, bell pepper, onion, garlic, thyme, cinnamon, chocolate, and fresh cilantro. This high-protein meal is perfect for weight loss and will leave you feeling full and satisfied.

Servings: 4

Prepping Time: 20 minutes

Cook Time: 40 minutes

Difficulty: Medium

Ingredients:

- ✓ 1 lb lean ground turkey
- ✓ 1 can of black beans, drained and 1 can white beans, drained
- ✓ 2 tomatoes, diced and 1 bell pepper, diced
- ✓ 1 onion, chopped

- ✓ 2 garlic cloves, minced
- ✓ 2 tsp thyme
- ✓ 1/2 tsp cinnamon
- ✓ 1 oz dark chocolate, finely chopped
- ✓ 2 tbsp fresh cilantro, chopped
- ✓ Salt and pepper to taste

Step-by-Step Preparation:

1. In a large pot, sauté the turkey until no longer pink.
2. Add onions, bell pepper, and garlic. Cook until softened.
3. Stir in the tomatoes, black and white beans, thyme, cinnamon, and chocolate. Let simmer for 30 minutes.
4. Season with salt and pepper, then garnish with fresh cilantro before serving.

Nutritional Facts: (Per serving)

- ❖ Calories: 350
- ❖ Protein: 30g
- ❖ Fat: 12g
- ❖ Carbs: 35g
- ❖ Fiber: 10g
- ❖ Sugar: 5g

Indulge in this savory and hearty Turkey Chili bursting with flavors and high-quality protein. Perfect for a lunch meal, this dish doesn't just cater to your taste buds and aids in your weight loss journey by keeping you satiated for extended periods. Enjoy!

Recipe 23: Zesty Orange Salmon With Stir Fried Garlic Asparagus

Dive into this delightful recipe of Zesty Orange Salmon with Stir Fried Garlic Asparagus. A perfect blend of savory and sweet, this high-protein, low-fat dish is ideal for weight loss and is packed with flavors that will tingle your taste buds.

Servings: 4

Prepping Time: 15 Minutes

Cook Time: 25 Minutes

Difficulty: Medium

Ingredients:

- ✓ 4 salmon fillets
- ✓ 2 oranges, juiced and zested
- ✓ 2 tablespoons honey
- ✓ 2 tablespoons soy sauce

- ✓ 4 cloves garlic, minced
- ✓ 1 bunch asparagus, trimmed
- ✓ 2 tablespoons olive oil
- ✓ Salt and pepper to taste

Step-by-Step Preparation:

1. Marinate the salmon fillets in orange juice, zest, honey, and soy sauce for 30 minutes.

2. Preheat the oven to 400°F (200°C) and bake the salmon for 20 minutes.

3. While salmon is baking, sauté garlic in olive oil until fragrant. Add asparagus, season with salt and pepper, and stir-fry until tender.

4. Serve the baked salmon with stir-fried asparagus on the side.

Nutritional Facts: (Per serving)

- ❖ Calories: 350 kcal
- ❖ Protein: 34 g
- ❖ Fat: 14 g
- ❖ Carbs: 18 g
- ❖ Fiber: 3 g
- ❖ Sugar: 12 g

Relish the satisfaction of a well-cooked, nutrient-packed meal with this Zesty Orange Salmon and Stir Fried Garlic Asparagus. It's not just a meal; it's a step towards a healthier, leaner you. Your weight loss journey has never tasted so good!

Recipe 24: Tuna Wraps With Cucumber Onion

Dive into a refreshing, high-protein meal perfect for your weight loss journey - Tuna Wraps with Cucumber, Onion, and Mayonnaise, paired with a crisp Tomato Salad. This lunch dish combines satisfying flavors with healthful ingredients to help you reach your wellness goals.

Servings: 4

Prepping Time: 15 Minutes

Cook Time: 0 Minutes (No cooking required)

Difficulty: Easy

Ingredients:

- ✓ 2 cans of Tuna (in water, drained)
- ✓ 1 Cucumber (sliced)
- ✓ 1 Red Onion (sliced)
- ✓ 1/2 cup Mayonnaise (light)
- ✓ 4 Whole grain Wraps

- ✓ 2 Tomatoes (diced)
- ✓ 1/2 Lemon (juiced)
- ✓ Salt and Pepper to taste

Step-by-Step Preparation:

1. Combine the tuna, cucumber, red onion, and Mayonnaise in a bowl. Mix well.

2. Lay out the whole grain wraps and evenly distribute the tuna mixture.

3. Roll the wraps carefully and cut them into desired pieces.

4. Mix the diced tomatoes with lemon juice, salt, and Pepper in another bowl to make the salad.

5. Serve the wraps with the tomato salad on the side.

Nutritional Facts: (Per serving)

- ❖ Calories: 300
- ❖ Protein: 25g
- ❖ Fat: 12g (2g Saturated)
- ❖ Carbohydrates: 24g
- ❖ Dietary Fiber: 5g
- ❖ Sodium: 420mg

Relish the wholesome goodness of this high-protein Tuna Wrap with Cucumber, Onion, and Mayonnaise alongside a tangy Tomato Salad. It's a quick, no-cook dish with a weight-loss-friendly mix of nutrients and delightful flavors. Enjoy this refreshing lunch that helps you maintain your health without compromising taste.

Recipe 25: Peppers Stuffed With Quinoa and Walnuts

Introduce your taste buds to this delightful, nutrient-packed dish, "Peppers Stuffed with Quinoa and Walnuts." High in protein and fiber, it's an ideal lunch option for anyone pursuing weight loss without compromising flavor or satisfaction.

Servings: 4

Prepping Time: 20 Minutes

Cook Time: 35 Minutes

Difficulty: Intermediate

Ingredients:

- ✓ 4 large bell peppers
- ✓ 1 cup cooked quinoa
- ✓ 1 cup chopped walnuts
- ✓ 1/2 cup chopped onions

- ✓ 2 cloves garlic, minced
- ✓ 1 cup diced tomatoes and 1 teaspoon olive oil
- ✓ Salt and pepper to taste
- ✓ Fresh parsley for garnish

Step-by-Step Preparation:

1. Preheat the oven to 375°F (190°C).
2. Cut off the tops of the peppers and remove the seeds.
3. Heat the olive oil in a pan, add onions and garlic, and sauté until golden.
4. Add cooked quinoa, walnuts, tomatoes, salt, and pepper. Stir well.
5. Stuff the peppers with the quinoa mixture and place them on a baking tray.
6. Bake for 30-35 minutes or until peppers are tender.
7. Garnish with fresh parsley before serving.

Nutritional Facts: (Per serving)

- ❖ Calories: 300
- ❖ Protein: 10g
- ❖ Carbs: 35g
- ❖ Fiber: 7g
- ❖ Fat: 14g
- ❖ Sugars: 6g

With "Peppers Stuffed with Quinoa and Walnuts," enjoy a hearty, protein-rich meal that not only aids in weight loss but also ensures you're feeding your body quality nutrition. Dive into this colorful, mouthwatering dish and make your weight loss journey delicious.

Recipe 26: Caesar Roll With Chicken

Dive into a light yet protein-packed lunch with this Caesar Roll with Chicken. Perfectly grilled chicken, crisp lettuce, and a delightful Caesar dressing, all wrapped in a delicious roll, this dish will satisfy your taste buds while supporting your weight loss goals.

Servings: 4

Prepping Time: 15 Minutes

Cook Time: 20 Minutes

Difficulty: Easy

Ingredients:

- ✓ 4 bread rolls, preferably whole grain
- ✓ 2 chicken breasts, grilled and sliced
- ✓ 8 leaves romaine lettuce
- ✓ 2 tablespoons light Caesar dressing
- ✓ 2 tablespoons grated parmesan cheese

✓ Salt and pepper to taste

Step-by-Step Preparation:

1. Preheat your grill and cook chicken breasts until no longer pink, about 20 minutes.

2. Slice your bread rolls and spread Caesar dressing evenly on each half.

3. Distribute the grilled chicken slices and lettuce among the rolls.

4. Sprinkle with parmesan, salt, and pepper.

5. Serve immediately or wrap for a grab-and-go lunch.

Nutritional Facts: (Per serving)

❖ Calories: 340

❖ Protein: 30g

❖ Carbs: 30g

❖ Fat: 10g

❖ Fiber: 4g

❖ Sugar: 3g

Treat yourself to a delectable Caesar Roll with Chicken that's rich in protein and taste. This dish offers satiety without compromising on flavor, ideal for a weight loss lunch. Easy to prepare and even easier to enjoy, it's your answer to a nutritious, guilt-free meal.

Recipe 27: Home-Cooked Dish, Stir-Fried Pork Belly With Celery

Revitalize your lunch menu with this flavor-packed, healthy recipe of Stir-Fried Pork Belly with Celery. High in protein and low in carbs, it's an ideal choice for those on a weight loss journey or looking for a balanced diet.

Servings: 4

Prepping Time: 15 Minutes

Cook Time: 20 Minutes

Difficulty: Easy

Ingredients:

- ✓ 400g pork belly, thinly sliced
- ✓ 4 celery stalks, sliced
- ✓ 2 tablespoons soy sauce
- ✓ 1 tablespoon sesame oil
- ✓ 2 cloves garlic, minced

✓ 1 teaspoon ginger, grated

✓ Salt and pepper to taste

✓ 2 tablespoons olive oil

Step-by-Step Preparation:

1. Heat olive oil in a pan over medium heat.

2. Add pork belly and stir-fry until browned and crispy. Remove and set aside.

3. In the same pan, add garlic and ginger, and stir until fragrant.

4. Add celery, and stir-fry until slightly softened.

5. Return pork belly to the pan, add soy sauce, sesame oil, salt, and pepper. Stir-fry for another 5 minutes. Serve hot.

Nutritional Facts: (Per serving)

❖ Calories: 350

❖ Protein: 28g

❖ Fat: 25g

❖ Carbohydrates: 6g

❖ Fiber: 2g

❖ Sugar: 2g

Treat yourself to a protein-rich, mouthwatering lunch that's as delicious as it is nutritious. This Stir-Fried Pork Belly with Celery offers a quick, easy, and balanced meal, making it an excellent choice for anyone wishing to maintain a healthy lifestyle without compromising taste.

Recipe 28: Wild and Brown Rice With Seafood and Broccoli

Experience the ultimate blend of heartiness and health with this flavorful Wild and Brown Rice dish with Seafood and Broccoli. This protein-packed, low-fat lunch meal is your perfect weight-loss partner, enriched with fiber, vitamins, and heart-healthy omega-3 fatty acids.

Servings: 4

Prepping Time: 15 minutes

Cook Time: 35 minutes

Difficulty: Medium

Ingredients:

- ✓ 1 cup wild rice
- ✓ 1 cup brown rice
- ✓ 2 cups mixed seafood (shrimp, scallops, mussels)
- ✓ 2 cups broccoli florets

- ✓ 2 cloves garlic, minced
- ✓ 1 tablespoon olive oil
- ✓ Salt and pepper to taste
- ✓ Fresh lemon juice for serving

Step-by-Step Preparation:

1. Start cooking wild and brown rice in separate pots per the package instructions.

2. Heat olive oil over medium heat in a large pan, then add the garlic and cook until fragrant.

3. Add the mixed seafood and cook until it's completely done.

4. Add the broccoli florets, season with salt and pepper, and sauté until tender.

5. Combine the cooked rice, seafood, and broccoli, mixing thoroughly.

6. Serve the dish hot, drizzled with fresh lemon juice for added zest.

Nutritional Facts: (Per serving)

- ❖ Calories: 345
- ❖ Protein: 26g
- ❖ Fat: 6g
- ❖ Carbs: 50g
- ❖ Fiber: 6g
- ❖ Sugar: 2g

The Wild and Brown Rice with Seafood and Broccoli dish is your go-to nutritious, delicious, and satisfying meal. This balanced recipe will keep you full and satisfied and help you in your weight loss journey by providing a high-protein, low-fat, and fiber-rich lunch option.

Recipe 29: Baked Tilapia Served With Arugula and Quinoa Salad

Delight your senses and support your weight loss goals with this light, nutritious, high-protein Baked Tilapia served with Arugula and Quinoa Salad. This vibrant, flavorful dish pairs tender tilapia with a hearty salad for a meal that's as satisfying as it is healthy.

Servings: 4

Prepping Time: 20 minutes

Cook Time: 25 minutes

Difficulty: Easy

Ingredients:

- ✓ 4 tilapia fillets
- ✓ 2 tbsp olive oil
- ✓ Salt and pepper to taste
- ✓ 1 cup quinoa

- ✓ 2 cups water
- ✓ 4 cups arugula
- ✓ 1 lemon
- ✓ 1/4 cup feta cheese
- ✓ 1/2 cup cherry tomatoes

Step-by-Step Preparation:

1. Preheat the oven to 400°F. Season the tilapia fillets with olive oil, salt, and pepper, then bake for 15-20 minutes.

2. In a saucepan, bring quinoa and water to a boil. Reduce heat, cover, and simmer for 15 minutes.

3. Toss the cooked quinoa with arugula, lemon juice, feta cheese, and cherry tomatoes.

4. Serve the baked tilapia on a bed of the salad.

Nutritional Facts: (Per serving)

- ❖ Calories: 325
- ❖ Protein: 30g
- ❖ Carbs: 30g
- ❖ Fiber: 4g
- ❖ Fat: 9g

Revel in the healthful combination of lean protein and nutrient-rich ingredients in this Baked Tilapia with Arugula and Quinoa Salad. This dish is perfect for those seeking a delicious, high-protein meal that not only aids in weight loss but also tantalizes the tastebuds.

Recipe 30: Jacket Baked Potato With Tomato Beans, Cheddar Cheese

Reignite your lunchtime routine with this nutritious and satisfying high-protein Jacket Baked Potato with Tomato Beans and Cheddar Cheese. This balanced meal is designed to help you lose weight while delighting your taste buds.

Servings: 4

Prepping Time: 10 minutes

Cook Time: 60 minutes

Difficulty: Easy

Ingredients:

- ✓ 4 large baking potatoes
- ✓ 2 cups canned baked beans in tomato sauce
- ✓ 1 cup shredded cheddar cheese
- ✓ Salt and pepper, to taste

✓ Olive oil

Step-by-Step Preparation:

1. Preheat oven to 400°F. Prick potatoes with a fork and rub with olive oil.

2. Place potatoes in the oven and bake for 1 hour or until soft.

3. Heat beans in a saucepan until warm.

4. Cut open each baked potato. Season with salt and pepper.

5. Spoon beans into each potato and top with shredded cheese.

6. Serve hot.

Nutritional Facts: (Per serving)

❖ Calories: 450

❖ Protein: 20g

❖ Carbohydrates: 65g

❖ Dietary Fiber: 10g

❖ Fat: 10g

❖ Cholesterol: 30mg

Dive into this delicious Jacket Baked Potato with Tomato Beans and Cheddar Cheese dish - a quintessential comfort food with a high-protein twist. Perfect for those looking to maintain a balanced diet without sacrificing flavor. Enjoy this meal as a delightful part of your weight-loss journey.

Chapter 04: Afternoon Protein Snacks

Recipe 31: Sriracha Deviled Eggs With Different Toppings

Welcome to the vibrant, spicy, protein-packed world of Sriracha Deviled Eggs with Different Toppings. A fantastic, high-protein, low-calorie afternoon snack that fuels your weight-loss journey. This dish delivers a fiery kick and a variety of delightful textures, taking the classic deviled egg to the next level.

Servings: 4

Prepping Time: 15 minutes

Cook Time: 12 minutes

Difficulty: Easy

Ingredients:

- ✓   8 large eggs

- ✓ 1/3 cup mayonnaise

- ✓ 2 tablespoons Sriracha sauce

- ✓ 1 teaspoon white vinegar

- ✓ Salt and pepper to taste

- ✓ Toppings: Fresh herbs, chopped bacon, and sesame seeds

Step-by-Step Preparation:

1. Hard boil the eggs, cool, peel, and cut in half lengthwise.

2. Remove the yolks, mix with mayo, Sriracha, vinegar, salt, and pepper until smooth.

3. Refill each egg white with the yolk mixture.

4. Garnish with your choice of toppings.

Nutritional Facts: (Per serving)

- ❖ Calories: 210

- ❖ Protein: 12g

- ❖ Carbs: 2g

- ❖ Fat: 16g

- ❖ Fiber: 0g

Reinvent your afternoon snack routine with these Sriracha Deviled Eggs, offering a symphony of flavors, all while supporting your weight loss goals. This easy-to-make, protein-rich dish satisfies your taste buds and keeps you satiated, assisting your journey toward a healthier lifestyle.

Recipe 32: Roasted Spicy Chickpeas

Welcome to a quick, protein-packed snack recipe perfect for weight loss – Roasted Spicy Chickpeas. Crunchy, spicy, and nutrition-dense, these chickpeas are an excellent pick-me-up for your afternoon cravings.

Servings: 4

Prepping Time: 10 Minutes

Cook Time: 40 Minutes

Difficulty: Easy

Ingredients:

- ✓ 2 cans (15 ounces each) of chickpeas
- ✓ 1 tablespoon olive oil
- ✓ 1 teaspoon smoked paprika
- ✓ 1/2 teaspoon cayenne pepper
- ✓ Salt to taste

Step-by-Step Preparation:

1. Preheat your oven to 400°F (200°C). Drain, rinse, and dry chickpeas thoroughly.

2. Toss chickpeas with olive oil, smoked paprika, cayenne pepper, and salt.

3. Spread evenly on a baking sheet and roast for 30-40 minutes, stirring occasionally until crisp.

Nutritional Facts: (Per serving)

- ❖ Calories: 215

- ❖ Protein: 11g

- ❖ Carbs: 27g

- ❖ Fat: 7g

- ❖ Fiber: 9g

Take control of your health and enjoy these Roasted Spicy Chickpeas' spicy, flavorful kick. Whether you want to lose weight or seek a healthy snack, this recipe checks all the boxes while satisfying your taste buds.

Recipe 33: Granola With Yogurt and Fresh Berries

Kickstart your weight loss journey with this high-protein homemade granola with yogurt and fresh berries. This quick and easy snack keeps you feeling full while providing your body with essential nutrients.

Servings: 4

Prepping Time: 15 minutes

Cook Time: 25 minutes

Difficulty: Easy

Ingredients

- ✓ 2 cups old-fashioned oats
- ✓ 1 cup mixed nuts, chopped
- ✓ 2 tablespoons honey
- ✓ 1 tablespoon coconut oil
- ✓ 1/2 cup Greek yogurt

✓   1 cup fresh berries

Step-by-Step Preparation

1. Preheat your oven to 350°F.

2. Mix oats, nuts, honey, and coconut oil in a bowl. Spread on a baking sheet.

3. Bake for 20-25 minutes, until golden brown. Let it cool.

4. Add a layer of granola, Greek yogurt, and top with fresh berries in a bowl. Repeat layers if desired.

Nutritional Facts: (Per serving)

❖   Calories: 350 kcal

❖   Protein: 15g

❖   Carbohydrates: 45g

❖   Fat: 15g

❖   Fiber: 7g

This homemade granola bowl with yogurt and fresh berries is a delightful high-protein snack. Easy to make yet irresistibly delicious, it's the perfect afternoon pick-me-up for those on a weight loss journey, proving that healthy eating can be both satisfying and flavorsome.

Recipe 34: Healthy Honey Peanut Butter Date Walnut Protein Balls

Dive into the delicious, energy-packed world of "Healthy Honey Peanut Butter Date Walnut Protein Balls." This high-protein treat is perfect for those looking to lose weight or anyone needing an energy boost during the day.

Servings: 10

Prepping Time: 20 minutes

Cook Time: 0 minutes

Difficulty: Easy

Ingredients:

- ✓ 1 cup pitted dates
- ✓ 1 cup walnuts
- ✓ 1/2 cup natural peanut butter
- ✓ 2 tablespoons honey

- ✓ 1/4 cup protein powder (optional)
- ✓ Pinch of salt

Step-by-Step Preparation:

1. Blend the dates and walnuts in a food processor until finely chopped.

2. Add peanut butter, honey, protein powder (if using), and salt. Blend until a sticky mixture forms.

3. Roll the mixture into 10 balls using your hands.

4. Place the balls in the fridge for an hour to firm up.

Nutritional Facts: (Per serving)

- ❖ Calories: 200
- ❖ Protein: 8g
- ❖ Carbohydrates: 22g
- ❖ Fat: 10g
- ❖ Fiber: 3g
- ❖ Sugar: 18g

Indulge in the wholesome goodness of these "Healthy Honey Peanut Butter Date Walnut Protein Balls." They will satiate your afternoon cravings and provide you with a much-needed energy and protein boost, assisting you in your weight loss journey. Now, snack time will always be different!

Recipe 35: Slices of Bread With Cottage Cheese and Cherry Tomatoes

Dive into a world of flavor with these High-Protein Slices of Bread with Cottage Cheese and Cherry Tomatoes - an ideal weight-loss snack for your afternoon cravings. This recipe combines simplicity, health, and taste and provides fresh, vibrant flavors in every bite.

Servings: 2

Prepping Time: 10 minutes

Cook Time: 0 minutes

Difficulty: Easy

Ingredients:

- ✓   4 slices of whole-grain bread
- ✓   1 cup of cottage cheese
- ✓   1 cup of cherry tomatoes
- ✓   Salt and pepper to taste

✓ Fresh basil leaves for garnish

Step-by-Step Preparation:

1. Spread an equal amount of cottage cheese over each slice of bread.

2. Halve the cherry tomatoes and place them on top of the cottage cheese.

3. Sprinkle with salt and pepper to taste.

4. Garnish each slice with fresh basil leaves and serve.

Nutritional Facts: (Per serving)

❖ Calories: 220

❖ Protein: 16g

❖ Carbs: 27g

❖ Fiber: 4g

❖ Fat: 5g

❖ Sugar: 6g

Re-energize your afternoons with this delectable, high-protein snack, perfect for anyone looking to lose weight. Enjoy the balance of creamy cottage cheese, crunchy bread, and fresh tomatoes while benefiting from its wholesome nutrition. A delightful bite, brimming with health and flavor.

Recipe 36: Healthy Rice Cakes With Cherry Tomatoes

Savor the vibrant flavors of Healthy Rice Cakes topped with juicy cherry tomatoes, crumbled feta cheese, aromatic basil, and a sprinkle of sesame seeds. This high-protein afternoon snack will aid your weight loss journey while offering a tasty treat to your palate.

Servings: 2

Prepping Time: 10 minutes

Cook Time: 0 minutes

Difficulty: Easy

Ingredients:

- ✓ 4 rice cakes
- ✓ 1 cup cherry tomatoes, halved
- ✓ 1/2 cup feta cheese, crumbled
- ✓ 2 tablespoons fresh basil, chopped

✓ 1 tablespoon sesame seeds

Step-by-Step Preparation:

1. Lay out the rice cakes on a flat surface.

2. Top each rice cake with an even distribution of cherry tomatoes.

3. Sprinkle feta cheese on top of the tomatoes.

4. Garnish with chopped basil.

5. Finish by sprinkling sesame seeds over each rice cake.

6. Serve immediately and enjoy!

Nutritional Facts: (Per serving)

❖ Calories: 200 kcal

❖ Protein: 8 g

❖ Fat: 9 g

❖ Carbohydrates: 23 g

❖ Dietary fiber: 2 g

❖ Sugars: 3 g

Delight in the refreshingly light and crunchy taste of these Healthy Rice Cakes. Simple to prepare and fulfill your appetite, this is a perfect choice for a health-conscious snack that doesn't compromise flavor. Recharge your afternoon while maintaining your weight loss goals with this protein-rich dish.

Recipe 37: Fried Zucchini Sticks and Tomato Sauce

Indulge in the crunchy goodness of Fried Zucchini Sticks paired with a tangy Tomato Sauce - a perfect high-protein afternoon snack. This low-calorie recipe is excellent for your weight loss journey, blending taste with nutrition.

Servings: 4

Prepping Time: 15 minutes

Cook Time: 15 minutes

Difficulty: Easy

Ingredients:

- ✓ 2 large zucchinis
- ✓ 1 cup whole wheat breadcrumbs
- ✓ 1/2 cup parmesan cheese, grated
- ✓ 2 eggs, beaten
- ✓ Salt and pepper to taste

- ✓ 1 cup tomato sauce
- ✓ Fresh basil leaves for garnish

Step-by-Step Preparation:

1. Cut zucchini into sticks.

2. In a bowl, mix breadcrumbs and parmesan.

3. Dip each zucchini stick into beaten eggs, then coat with breadcrumb mixture.

4. Fry in a non-stick pan until golden brown.

5. Serve with warmed tomato sauce and garnish with fresh basil.

Nutritional Facts: (Per serving)

- ❖ Calories: 220

- ❖ Protein: 13g

- ❖ Carbohydrates: 28g

- ❖ Fat: 7g

- ❖ Fiber: 5g

- ❖ Sugar: 6g

Recharge your afternoons with these delectable Fried Zucchini Sticks. They're crunchy, nutritious, and full of protein to keep you satisfied and aid in your weight loss goals. This easy recipe will soon become your go-to snack, merging health with indulgence.

Recipe 38: Avocado Hummus With Zucchini Bell Pepper Veggie Sticks

Step into a world of delectable green goodness with this Avocado Hummus With Zucchini Bell Pepper Veggie Sticks. This afternoon snack, rich in high-quality plant proteins, will keep you full while supporting your weight loss goals.

Servings: 4

Prepping Time: 15 minutes

Cook Time: N/A

Difficulty: Easy

Ingredients:

- ✓ 2 ripe avocados
- ✓ 1 can chickpeas, drained
- ✓ 2 cloves garlic
- ✓ 1 lemon, juiced

- ✓ 2 tablespoons tahini
- ✓ 2 tablespoons olive oil
- ✓ Salt to taste
- ✓ 1 zucchini, cut into sticks
- ✓ 1 bell pepper, cut into sticks

Step-by-Step Preparation:

1. Combine the avocados, chickpeas, garlic, lemon juice, tahini, olive oil, and salt in a food processor.
2. Blend until smooth, adding water if necessary for desired consistency.
3. Serve the avocado hummus with the zucchini and bell pepper sticks.

Nutritional Facts: (Per serving)

- ❖ Calories: 280
- ❖ Protein: 9g
- ❖ Fat: 20g
- ❖ Carbohydrates: 22g
- ❖ Dietary Fiber: 10g

Elevate your afternoon snack routine with this nutritionally-balanced Avocado Hummus With Zucchini Bell Pepper Veggie Sticks. Indulge in the creamy hummus paired with crunchy veggie sticks while fueling your body with essential nutrients and aiding your weight loss journey.

Recipe 39: Flat-Lay of Vegan Wholegrain Toasts With Fruit

Delight in the satisfying crunch of Vegan Wholegrain toast, an ideal high-protein weight-loss snack. Adorned with an array of fruits, seeds, nuts, and a smear of peanut butter paired perfectly with a rich cup of espresso. This treat is nourishing, easy to prepare, and a testament to delicious and healthful eating.

Servings: 2

Prepping Time: 10 minutes

Cook Time: 5 minutes

Difficulty: Easy

Ingredients:

- ✓ 4 slices of wholegrain bread
- ✓ 2 tablespoons of peanut butter
- ✓ 1 banana, sliced
- ✓ Handful of mixed seeds (pumpkin, flax, sesame)

- ✓ Handful of mixed nuts (walnuts, almonds)
- ✓ 1 apple, sliced
- ✓ 1 cup of espresso

Step-by-Step Preparation:

1. Toast the wholegrain bread to your liking.
2. Spread peanut butter evenly on each toast.
3. Arrange the sliced fruits, seeds, and nuts on top.
4. Brew and serve the espresso in a cup.
5. Enjoy this healthy, protein-packed snack with your coffee.

Nutritional Facts: (Per serving)

- ❖ Calories: 300
- ❖ Protein: 15g
- ❖ Carbohydrates: 35g
- ❖ Fat: 13g
- ❖ Fiber: 7g
- ❖ Sugar: 12g

Feast your senses on this appealing and energizing Vegan Wholegrain Toast, ideal for an afternoon pick-me-up. Replete with a balance of proteins, fibers, and healthy fats, it supports weight loss while satisfying your cravings. Accompanied by a full-bodied espresso, it makes a delightful pairing that will surely lift your spirits.

Recipe 40: Spicy Grilled Edamame Soy Beans With Sea Salt

Revitalize your afternoon snacking with the Spicy Grilled Edamame Soy Beans with Sea Salt recipe. Offering a high-protein punch fiery yet balanced dish supports weight loss and keeps hunger pangs at bay while adding an enticing flavor to your day.

Servings: 4

Prepping Time: 10 minutes

Cook Time: 15 minutes

Difficulty: Easy

Ingredients:

- ✓ 2 cups fresh edamame
- ✓ 2 tablespoons olive oil
- ✓ 1 teaspoon sea salt
- ✓ 1/2 teaspoon chili flakes

Step-by-Step Preparation:

1. Preheat your grill to medium heat.

2. Toss the edamame in olive oil, sea salt, and chili flakes.

3. Grill for about 15 minutes, turning occasionally until slightly charred.

4. Serve warm, and enjoy!

Nutritional Facts: (Per serving)

❖ Calories: 190 kcal

❖ Protein: 17g

❖ Carbs: 9g

❖ Fat: 10g

❖ Sodium: 590mg

Indulge in the Spicy Grilled Edamame Soy Beans with Sea Salt for a gratifying, high-protein snack. This simple, flavorful, and health-conscious dish is perfect for those looking to lose weight or just seeking a delicious, energizing treat for their afternoon. Your tastebuds and waistline will thank you.

Chapter 05: End the Day Right High-Protein Dinners

Recipe 41: Fried Rice With Tamarind Paste

Immerse yourself in the rich flavors of Thai cuisine with "Fried Rice with Tamarind Paste, Chinese Sausage and Salted Egg and Vegetables - Khao pad Nam Prig Ma-kham, Chilli Tamarind Sauce Dip." This exquisite blend offers a high-protein meal perfect for weight-loss dinners.

Servings: 4

Prepping Time: 15 minutes

Cook Time: 30 minutes

Difficulty: Intermediate

Ingredients:

- ✓   2 cups of cooked jasmine rice

- ✓   4 Chinese sausages, thinly sliced

- ✓ 2 salted eggs, chopped
- ✓ 1 cup of mixed vegetables (carrot, peas, corn)
- ✓ 4 tablespoons of tamarind paste and 2 tablespoons of fish sauce
- ✓ 2 cloves of garlic, minced and 2 tablespoons of vegetable oil
- ✓ 2 red chilies, finely chopped and Fresh cilantro for garnish

Step-by-Step Preparation:

1. Heat oil in a wok or large frying pan over medium heat.
2. Add garlic and sauté until golden.
3. Stir in Chinese sausage and cook until browned.
4. Add mixed vegetables, stirring until they soften.
5. Add the cooked rice and mix well.
6. Mix in tamarind paste and fish sauce, stirring until well combined.
7. Add chopped salted eggs, stirring gently.
8. Garnish with chopped chilies and cilantro before serving.

Nutritional Facts: (Per serving)

- ❖ Calories: 350
- ❖ Protein: 22g
- ❖ Carbs: 40g
- ❖ Fat: 12g
- ❖ Sodium: 600mg
- ❖ Fiber: 4g

Fusing the exotic sweetness of tamarind paste, the savory essence of Chinese sausage, and the unique flavor of salted egg, this fried rice variant is a feast for the palate and a nourishing high-protein meal for your weight loss journey. Enjoy the vibrant tastes of Thailand in every bite!

Recipe 42: Chicken Breast With Couscous and Vegetables

This Chicken Breast with Couscous and vegetable dish is a delicious, high-protein, weight-loss-friendly meal. A satisfying dinner is bursting with flavors and packed with lean protein, healthy carbs, and fiber to keep you full and fueled.

Servings: 4

Prepping Time: 15 Minutes

Cook Time: 30 Minutes

Difficulty: Easy

Ingredients:

- ✓   4 Boneless skinless chicken breasts
- ✓   1 cup of Couscous
- ✓   2 cups of Mixed vegetables (broccoli, bell peppers, carrots)
- ✓   2 tbsp Olive oil

- ✓ Salt and pepper to taste

- ✓ 1 tbsp Garlic powder

- ✓ Fresh herbs for garnish (parsley, thyme)

Step-by-Step Preparation:

1. Season the chicken breasts with salt, pepper, and garlic powder.

2. Heat the olive oil over medium heat and cook the chicken breasts until golden brown.

3. In the meantime, cook the couscous according to the package instructions.

4. Steam the vegetables until they're tender.

5. Once everything is cooked, assemble the dish by adding couscous, vegetables, and chicken breast to a plate.

6. Garnish with fresh herbs and serve warm.

Nutritional Facts: (Per serving)

- ❖ Calories: 450

- ❖ Protein: 35g

- ❖ Carbs: 40g

- ❖ Fiber: 5g

- ❖ Fat: 15g

Savor this Chicken Breast with Couscous and a vegetable dish to help fuel your weight loss journey. This meal is high in protein and has a perfect balance of good carbs and fiber, making it an ideal choice for a satisfying, nutrient-dense dinner.

Recipe 43: Traditional Fried and Stirred Crispy Tofu

Start your weight loss journey by enjoying this tasty, high-protein traditional crispy tofu stir-fry. Sauteed with soy sauce and pepper meal offers a mouthwatering blend of flavors, perfect for dinner. The crisp texture and aromatic spices make it irresistible.

Servings: 4

Prepping Time: 15 minutes

Cook Time: 20 minutes

Difficulty: Easy

Ingredients:

- ✓ 400 grams of firm tofu

- ✓ 2 tablespoons of vegetable oil

- ✓ 3 tablespoons of soy sauce

- ✓ 1 teaspoon of black pepper

- ✓ 2 garlic cloves, minced
- ✓ 1 small onion, finely chopped
- ✓ Chopped spring onions for garnish

Step-by-Step Preparation:

1. Drain and press tofu to remove excess water. Cut into bite-sized cubes.

2. Heat vegetable oil in a pan over medium heat. Add tofu cubes and fry until golden brown.

3. Remove tofu and set aside. In the same pan, sauté garlic and onion until fragrant.

4. Return tofu to the pan, add soy sauce and black pepper. Stir fry for a few minutes until tofu absorbs the flavors.

5. Serve hot, garnished with spring onions.

Nutritional Facts: (Per serving)

- ❖ Calories: 200
- ❖ Protein: 12g
- ❖ Fat: 13g
- ❖ Carbohydrates: 9g
- ❖ Fiber: 2g
- ❖ Sodium: 800mg

End your day with this protein-rich crispy tofu stir-fry, a perfect combination of taste and health. It's a feast for the palate and a nutritious meal to aid your weight loss. Enjoy this delightful dinner that won't compromise your health goals.

Recipe 44: Turkey Meatballs With Zucchini Noodles

Enjoy a tasty, healthy spin on traditional spaghetti and meatballs with our high-protein Turkey Meatballs with Zucchini Noodles recipe. It's a satisfying meal to help you stay on track with your weight loss goals without sacrificing flavor.

Servings: 4

Prepping Time: 20 minutes

Cook Time: 30 minutes

Difficulty: Easy

Ingredients:

- ✓ 1 lb lean ground turkey
- ✓ 1/4 cup whole wheat breadcrumbs
- ✓ 1 large egg and 2 cloves garlic, minced
- ✓ 1/2 tsp salt and 1/2 tsp black pepper

- ✓ 4 large zucchinis, spiralized and 1 cup marinara sauce
- ✓ 2 tbsp olive oil and 1/4 cup grated Parmesan cheese
- ✓ Fresh basil for garnish

Step-by-Step Preparation:

1. Mix turkey, breadcrumbs, egg, garlic, salt, and pepper in a bowl. Form into meatballs.

2. Heat oil in a pan, add meatballs and cook until browned and cooked. Remove and set aside.

3. In the same pan, add zucchini noodles and cook for 2-3 minutes, just until tender.

4. Add marinara sauce to the pan, and stir well. Return meatballs to the pan and heat through.

5. Serve hot, topped with Parmesan cheese and fresh basil.

Nutritional Facts: (Per serving)

- ❖ Calories: 300
- ❖ Protein: 30g
- ❖ Carbs: 15g
- ❖ Fiber: 4g
- ❖ Fat: 13g
- ❖ Sugar: 7g

Revamp your dinner routine with this nutritious, mouthwatering Turkey Meatballs with Zucchini Noodles. Perfect for those aiming for weight loss, it delivers high protein content to keep you feeling full while treating your taste buds to a delicious meal. Say goodbye to bland diet foods and hello to flavorful, healthy eating!

Recipe 45: Grilled Salmon With Quinoa

Experience the perfect balance of nutrition and flavor with this Grilled Salmon with Quinoa, Pumpkin Puree, and Grilled Asparagus dish. High in protein, this meal promotes weight loss while delivering a satisfying, gourmet dining experience.

Servings: 4

Prepping Time: 15 minutes

Cook Time: 30 minutes

Difficulty: Intermediate

Ingredients:

- ✓ 4 Salmon fillets
- ✓ 2 cups Quinoa
- ✓ 1 small Pumpkin
- ✓ 1 bunch Asparagus
- ✓ Olive oil

- ✓ Salt and pepper
- ✓ Fresh parsley for garnish

Step-by-Step Preparation:

1. Rinse and cook quinoa according to package instructions.

2. Halve and roast pumpkin at 200°C until soft, then puree in a blender.

3. Season salmon fillets and asparagus with olive oil, salt, and pepper, then grill each side for 4-5 minutes.

4. Plate quinoa, top with salmon, and serve with pumpkin puree and grilled asparagus.

5. Garnish with fresh parsley.

Nutritional Facts: (Per serving)

- ❖ Calories: 560 kcal

- ❖ Protein: 40g

- ❖ Carbohydrates: 55g

- ❖ Fiber: 6g

- ❖ Fat: 20g

Revamp your dinner routine with this health-focused, delectable Grilled Salmon with Quinoa, Pumpkin Puree, and Grilled Asparagus dish. High in protein, packed with essential nutrients, and subtly nuanced with flavors, it's the ideal choice for weight loss or those seeking a nutritious, delicious meal.

Recipe 46: Salmon With Quinoa and Omega 3 Seeds

Embark on a nourishing culinary adventure with this healthy, high-protein meal - Salmon with Quinoa and Omega 3 Seeds. It's not just delectable but a powerhouse of nutrients, perfect for weight loss dinners.

Servings: 4

Prepping Time: 15 Minutes

Cook Time: 30 Minutes

Difficulty: Intermediate

Ingredients:

- ✓ 4 salmon fillets

- ✓ 1 cup quinoa

- ✓ 2 cups water

- ✓ 2 tablespoons of Omega 3 seeds (flax, chia, hemp)

- ✓ 2 tablespoons olive oil

✓ Salt and pepper to taste

✓ Lemon wedges for serving

✓ Fresh herbs (dill, parsley) for garnish

Step-by-Step Preparation:

1. Preheat the oven to 375°F. Season salmon with salt, pepper, and olive oil. Bake for 15-20 minutes or until done to your liking.

2. While the salmon cooks, rinse the quinoa under cold water until the water clears. Boil quinoa in 2 cups of water until tender, about 15 minutes. Fluff with a fork.

3. Stir in the Omega 3 seeds into the cooked quinoa.

4. Plate the quinoa and top it with the baked salmon. Garnish with fresh herbs and serve with a lemon wedge.

Nutritional Facts: (Per serving)

❖ Calories: 490

❖ Protein: 40g

❖ Carbs: 30g

❖ Fat: 20g (healthy fats from Omega 3 seeds)

❖ Fiber: 5g

Relish this delectable Salmon with Quinoa and Omega 3 Seeds dish, packed with protein and the heart-healthy goodness of Omega 3. It's an exquisite blend of taste and health, giving your weight loss journey a delicious twist. Stay fit, stay satiated!

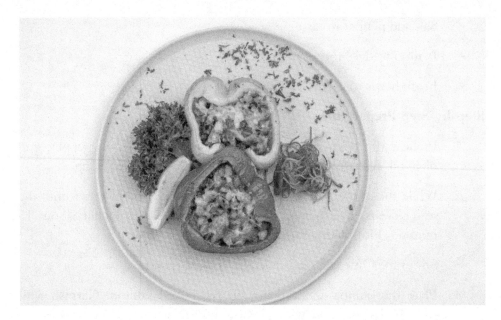

Recipe 47: Bell Pepper Stuffed Chicken Fajita Meal

Dive into a colorful and nutritious dinner with this Bell Pepper Stuffed Chicken Fajita Meal. High in protein, it's perfect for weight loss and deliciously satisfying. The bell peppers add a crunch, the chicken ensures lean protein, and the fajita seasoning brings the heat, making every bite an adventure.

Servings: 4

Prepping Time: 20 minutes

Cook Time: 25 minutes

Difficulty: Easy

Ingredients:

- ✓ 4 bell peppers (red, yellow, and green), hollowed
- ✓ 2 chicken breasts, sliced
- ✓ 2 tablespoons olive oil
- ✓ 1 packet of fajita seasoning

- ✓ 1 onion, sliced
- ✓ 2 cloves garlic, minced
- ✓ 1 cup shredded cheese
- ✓ Salt and pepper to taste

Step-by-Step Preparation:

1. Preheat oven to 375°F.

2. In a pan, heat oil, add chicken, onions, garlic, and fajita seasoning. Cook until the chicken is done.

3. Stuff bell peppers with the cooked chicken mixture, top with shredded cheese.

4. Bake stuffed peppers for 20-25 minutes or until the peppers are tender and the cheese is melted.

5. Allow to cool before serving.

Nutritional Facts: (Per serving)

- ❖ Calories: 350
- ❖ Protein: 28g
- ❖ Carbohydrates: 20g
- ❖ Fat: 15g
- ❖ Fiber: 4g
- ❖ Sodium: 600mg

Ditch the traditional fajitas and enjoy them stuffed in colorful bell peppers. This Bell Pepper Stuffed Chicken Fajita Meal offers a vibrant, high-protein, and low-carb solution for those evenings when you want a quick, delicious, and weight-loss-friendly dinner. It's as delightful to the eyes as it is to your taste buds.

Recipe 48: Grilled Pork Kebab

Relish this vibrant and flavorful Grilled Pork Kebab with Red and Yellow Pepper. It's a perfect weight loss dinner dish packed with high proteins and low in calories, offering a delightful blend of succulent pork and refreshing peppers.

Servings: 4

Prepping Time: 15 Minutes

Cook Time: 15 Minutes

Difficulty: Easy

Ingredients:

- ✓ 500g Pork Tenderloin, cubed
- ✓ 1 Red Bell Pepper, cubed
- ✓ 1 Yellow Bell Pepper, cubed
- ✓ 2 tbsp Olive Oil
- ✓ 1 tbsp Lemon Juice

- ✓ 2 Garlic Cloves, minced
- ✓ Salt and Pepper to taste
- ✓ Skewers

Step-by-Step Preparation:

1. Marinate the pork cubes with olive oil, lemon juice, garlic, salt, and Pepper. Let it rest for at least 30 minutes.

2. Preheat the grill to medium heat.

3. Skewer the pork and peppers alternately.

4. Grill the skewers for about 15 minutes or until the pork is fully cooked, turning occasionally.

5. Serve the kebabs hot.

Nutritional Facts: (Per serving)

- ❖ Calories: 300
- ❖ Proteins: 25g
- ❖ Carbohydrates: 10g
- ❖ Fats: 18g

Delicious and nutritious, our Grilled Pork Kebab with Red and Yellow Pepper is a winning weight-loss dinner choice. Its high protein content supports muscle health, while its delightful taste caters to your palate. Revamp your dinner routine with this protein-rich, guilt-free indulgence.

Recipe 49: Cream Coconut Lentil Curry With Rice and Naan Bread

Experience the magic of Indian cuisine with our Cream Coconut Lentil Curry served with fluffy rice and warm naan bread. A perfect combination of nutrition and taste, this high-protein meal aids in weight loss while satisfying your cravings for something savory and aromatic.

Servings: 4

Prepping Time: 20 minutes

Cook Time: 30 minutes

Difficulty: Intermediate

Ingredients:

- ✓ 1 cup of lentils
- ✓ 1 can of coconut milk
- ✓ 2 tablespoons of curry powder
- ✓ 2 cups of basmati rice

- ✓ 4 pieces of naan bread
- ✓ 1 onion, finely chopped
- ✓ 2 cloves of garlic, minced
- ✓ Salt and pepper to taste

Step-by-Step Preparation:

1. Rinse lentils and cook in a pot with water until soft.
2. In another pot, sauté onion and garlic until golden.
3. Add curry powder, coconut milk, and lentils to the pot, simmering for 15 minutes.
4. In the meantime, cook the basmati rice as per package instructions.
5. Warm naan bread in the oven for a few minutes.
6. Serve lentil curry over rice with a side of warm naan bread.

Nutritional Facts: (Per serving)

- ❖ Calories: 520
- ❖ Protein: 22g
- ❖ Carbohydrates: 68g
- ❖ Fat: 18g
- ❖ Fiber: 15g
- ❖ Sodium: 450mg

Relish in this wholesome Cream Coconut Lentil Curry, a dish that's as nourishing as it is delicious. The balanced protein and fiber content aids in weight loss, while the curry's rich flavors make it a delectable dinner option. Serve it up with rice and naan for an indulgent yet healthy treat!

Recipe 50: Stir Fry Pepper Chicken

Treat your taste buds to this hearty, high-protein Stir Fry Pepper Chicken. Packed with lean chicken, vibrant sweet peppers, onions, fragrant garlic, and zesty ginger, it's an indulgence that supports your weight loss journey without sacrificing flavor.

Servings: 4

Prepping Time: 15 Minutes

Cook Time: 20 Minutes

Difficulty: Easy

Ingredients:

- ✓ 500g boneless chicken breasts
- ✓ 3 sweet peppers (red, yellow, and green)
- ✓ 1 large onion
- ✓ 4 cloves garlic
- ✓ 1 tablespoon freshly grated ginger

- ✓ 2 tablespoons olive oil

- ✓ Salt and pepper to taste

- ✓ 2 tablespoons low-sodium soy sauce

- ✓ 1 teaspoon red pepper flakes (optional)

Step-by-Step Preparation:

1. Thinly slice chicken, peppers, and onion. Mince garlic and grate ginger.

2. In a large pan, heat olive oil over medium-high heat.

3. Add chicken and stir fry until no longer pink.

4. Add onions, sweet peppers, garlic, ginger, salt, and pepper. Stir fry until veggies are crisp-tender.

5. Drizzle soy sauce and sprinkle red pepper flakes. Stir well.

6. Cook for another 2-3 minutes until everything is well incorporated.

7. Serve hot.

Nutritional Facts: (Per serving)

- ❖ Calories: 300

- ❖ Protein: 35g

- ❖ Carbs: 15g

- ❖ Fiber: 3g

- ❖ Fat: 10g

- ❖ Sodium: 320mg

Savor this colorful, nutrient-dense Stir Fry Pepper Chicken, a meal satisfying your cravings and dietary goals. It's not just a dinner; it's a step forward in your weight loss journey, bringing you closer to a healthier, leaner you. Enjoy this dish that harmoniously blends taste and nutrition.

Chapter 06: Late-Night Cravings

←————————————————————————→

Recipe 51: Bowl of Greek Yogurt With Fresh Blueberries

Delve into a tasty midnight snack that aids weight loss with this protein-rich Greek yogurt bowl. Filled with fresh blueberries, crunchy almond pieces, and sweet honey simple dish delivers wholesome nourishment for late-night cravings.

Servings: 1

Prepping Time: 5 minutes

Cook Time: No cooking required

Difficulty: Easy

Ingredients:

- ✓ 1 cup Greek yogurt

- ✓ 1/2 cup fresh blueberries

- ✓ 1/4 cup almond pieces
- ✓ 1-2 tablespoons honey

Step-by-Step Preparation:

1. Pour Greek yogurt into a bowl.

2. Sprinkle fresh blueberries and almond pieces over the top.

3. Drizzle with honey to your preference.

4. Mix lightly to blend the flavors before digging in.

Nutritional Facts: (Per serving)

- ❖ Calories: 350 kcal

- ❖ Protein: 25 g

- ❖ Carbs: 28 g

- ❖ Fat: 14 g

- ❖ Fiber: 4 g

Delight in the perfect balance of sweet, tangy, and crunchy with this high-protein Greek yogurt bowl. This quick and easy-to-make dish fulfills your late-night munchies and aids in your weight loss journey by keeping you satiated until morning.

Recipe 52: Bread Texture of Sliced Home Baked Chocolate Roll

Indulge your late-night cravings with this delectable, high-protein Chocolate Babka with Apricots and a Cottage Cheese Roll with Peaches. With the perfect blend of sweet, savory, and richness, this is your go-to snack for weight loss that doesn't compromise flavor.

Servings: 4

Prepping Time: 45 minutes

Cook Time: 30 minutes

Difficulty: Medium

Ingredients:

- ✓ 2 cups of whole wheat flour
- ✓ 2 tablespoons of cocoa powder
- ✓ 1 tablespoon of instant yeast
- ✓ 1/2 cup of milk

- ✓ 2 tablespoons of honey

- ✓ 1 cup of dried apricots, chopped

- ✓ 1 cup of cottage cheese

- ✓ 2 peaches, pitted and thinly sliced

Step-by-Step Preparation:

1. Combine the flour, cocoa, and yeast. Add milk and honey, and knead until a smooth dough forms. Let it rise for 30 minutes.

2. Roll the dough out, sprinkle with apricots. Roll it up and place it in a greased loaf pan. Bake for 30 minutes at 180°C.

3. While babka bakes, blend cottage cheese until smooth. Spread it onto thinly sliced peaches and roll them up.

Nutritional Facts: (Per serving)

- ❖ Calories: 320

- ❖ Protein: 15g

- ❖ Carbohydrates: 55g

- ❖ Fat: 5g

- ❖ Fiber: 8g

Enjoy this irresistible, protein-rich midnight snack. The silky texture of the bread, the surprise of the apricots, and the contrasting fresh peach cottage cheese rolls create an exquisite combination, promising a satisfying, healthful indulgence. Every bite delivers a guilt-free pleasure, perfect for those late-night munchies.

Recipe 53: Chicken Rolls With Bacon and Creamy Filling

Kick-start your weight loss journey with this mouthwatering high-protein midnight snack. Relish the taste of tender chicken rolls stuffed with a creamy filling and wrapped in crispy bacon, all grilled to perfection. It's a delicious gourmet dish that you can quickly cook at home.

Servings: 4

Prepping Time: 15 minutes

Cook Time: 20 minutes

Difficulty: Intermediate

Ingredients:

- ✓ 4 boneless chicken breasts
- ✓ 8 slices of bacon
- ✓ 1 cup of cream cheese
- ✓ 1 cup of shredded cheddar cheese

- ✓ 2 green onions, chopped
- ✓ Salt and pepper to taste

Step-by-Step Preparation:

1. Flatten chicken breasts and season with salt and pepper.

2. Mix cream cheese, cheddar, and green onions. Spread the mixture onto each chicken breast.

3. Roll up each chicken breast, then wrap it with 2 slices of bacon.

4. Secure with toothpicks and grill on medium heat until the chicken is cooked and the bacon is crispy about 20 minutes.

Nutritional Facts: (Per serving)

- ❖ Calories: 520
- ❖ Protein: 42g
- ❖ Fat: 35g
- ❖ Carbs: 3g
- ❖ Fiber: 0g
- ❖ Sugar: 2g

Thanks to its high protein content, indulge in this delicious midnight treat without guilt. These grilled chicken rolls with bacon and creamy filling provide the right balance of nutrients, helping you meet your weight loss goals while keeping your taste buds delighted.

Recipe 54: Healthy Energy Protein Balls

Savor the indulgent flavors of these Healthy Energy Protein Balls. With a combination of dates, oats, peanut butter, and dark chocolate, these gluten-free truffle bites, coated with cocoa powder or almonds, offer a perfect balance of health and taste. Ideal as a high-protein weight loss midnight snack, it's delicious and straightforward to prepare.

Servings: 15 Balls

Prepping Time: 20 Minutes

Cook Time: No-Cook

Difficulty: Easy

Ingredients:

- ✓ 1 cup of Medjool dates, pitted
- ✓ 2 cups of rolled oats
- ✓ 1/2 cup of peanut butter
- ✓ 1/2 cup of dark chocolate, chopped
- ✓ 2 tablespoons of cocoa powder or crushed almonds for coating

Step-by-Step Preparation:

1. Blend the dates, oats, peanut butter, and dark chocolate in a food processor until a sticky mixture is formed.

2. Shape the mixture into balls using your hands.

3. Roll the balls in cocoa powder or crushed almonds for coating.

4. Refrigerate for at least 2 hours before serving.

Nutritional Facts: (Per serving)

❖ Calories: 155

❖ Protein: 5 grams

❖ Carbohydrates: 23 grams

❖ Fiber: 3 grams

❖ Fat: 6 grams

Incorporate these Healthy Energy Protein Balls into your diet as a midnight snack and enjoy their exquisite taste without compromising your weight loss goals. Not only will they satisfy your cravings, but they will also boost energy and protein, supporting your health journey most delightfully.

Recipe 55: Mini Shish Kofta Kofte Kebab

Indulge in these flavorful Mini Shish Kofta Kebab Canapes, a perfect high-protein midnight weight-loss snack. Packed with succulent meat and spices, they're a delightful way to satisfy your late-night cravings without sacrificing your fitness goals.

Servings: 4

Prepping Time: 20 minutes

Cook Time: 15 minutes

Difficulty: Medium

Ingredients:

- ✓ 500g lean minced meat
- ✓ 2 tbsp olive oil
- ✓ 2 cloves garlic, minced
- ✓ 1 onion, finely chopped
- ✓ 1 tsp ground cumin

- ✓ 1 tsp ground coriander
- ✓ Salt and pepper to taste
- ✓ Mini pita bread for serving
- ✓ Choice of dip (tzatziki, hummus, etc.)

Step-by-Step Preparation:

1. Mix minced meat, garlic, onion, spices, and seasoning in a bowl.

2. Shape the mixture into small, flat patties.

3. Heat oil in a pan, and cook patties until browned and cooked.

4. Serve on mini pita pieces of bread with your choice of dip.

Nutritional Facts: (Per serving)

- ❖ Calories: 320
- ❖ Protein: 30g
- ❖ Fat: 10g
- ❖ Carbohydrates: 20g
- ❖ Fiber: 2g
- ❖ Sugar: 3g

Reward your tastebuds without compromising your health with these Mini Shish Kofta Kebab Canapes. Enjoy the delicious blend of lean meat and spices, complemented by a tangy dip of your choice. It's the perfect dish to keep your late-night hunger at bay while maintaining a high-protein, low-carb diet.

Recipe 56: No Bake Protein Energy Balls With Strawberry

Elevate your midnight snacking experience with these No Bake Protein Energy Balls With Strawberries. These delightful, high-protein morsels help satisfy your sweet tooth while assisting in weight loss. No cooking is needed. Just combine, chill, and enjoy!

Servings: 15 Energy Balls

Prepping Time: 10 minutes

Cook Time: No Cooking Required

Difficulty: Easy

Ingredients:

- ✓ 1 cup oats
- ✓ ½ cup almond butter
- ✓ 2 scoops protein powder (vanilla)
- ✓ ¼ cup honey

- ✓ 1 cup dried strawberries, chopped
- ✓ 2 tablespoons chia seeds

Step-by-Step Preparation:

1. Mix oats, almond butter, protein powder, and honey in a large bowl until combined.

2. Add the dried strawberries and chia seeds. Mix until evenly distributed.

3. Roll the mixture into 15 small balls.

4. Refrigerate for at least an hour before serving to allow the balls to set.

Nutritional Facts: (Per serving)

- ❖ Calories: 120 kcal
- ❖ Protein: 7g
- ❖ Carbs: 10g
- ❖ Fat: 5g
- ❖ Fiber: 2g

These No Bake Protein Energy Balls With Strawberries perfectly fusion healthy and tasty. Ideal as a quick snack, for pre-workout fuel, or a post-dinner indulgence, these energy balls are high in protein, fiber, and flavor and low in prep time. Enjoy a guilt-free snack that also aids your weight loss journey.

Recipe 57: Healthy Wholefoods

Indulge in a satisfyingly sweet and nutritious midnight snack that fuels your weight loss journey. This high-protein dish with whole grain toast, peanut butter, bananas, fresh strawberries, almonds, and a drizzle of honey will keep your hunger and your health goals on track.

Servings: 2

Prepping Time: 10 Minutes

Cook Time: 5 Minutes

Difficulty: Easy

Ingredients:

- ✓ 4 slices of whole-grain toast
- ✓ 4 tablespoons of natural peanut butter
- ✓ 2 ripe bananas, sliced
- ✓ 8 fresh strawberries, sliced
- ✓ 1/4 cup of almonds, chopped

✓ 2 tablespoons of honey

Step-by-Step Preparation:

1. Toast the whole-grain bread to your preferred crispness.

2. Spread an even layer of peanut butter on each toast slice.

3. Top with banana and strawberry slices.

4. Sprinkle chopped almonds evenly across the slices.

5. Finish with a drizzle of honey and serve.

Nutritional Facts: (Per serving)

❖ Calories: 400

❖ Protein: 15g

❖ Carbohydrates: 50g

❖ Fat: 20g

❖ Fiber: 8g

❖ Sugar: 20g

High-protein toast is packed with natural ingredients and is perfect for curbing those late-night cravings while aiding weight loss. Healthy, flavorful, and easy to prepare, it's ideal for those seeking a nutritious snack without compromising taste or time. Enjoy this well-balanced and delectable treat that keeps you on a healthy path even after dark.

Recipe 58: Hummus Dip and Vegetables Sticks

Embark on a flavorful journey with this high-protein Hummus Dip and Vegetable Sticks recipe. Ideal for a weight loss midnight snack, it brings together the satiating goodness of protein-packed hummus and the crunch of fresh veggies.

Servings: 4

Prepping Time: 15 minutes

Cook Time: 0 minutes

Difficulty: Easy

Ingredients:

- ✓ 1 cup canned chickpeas
- ✓ 2 garlic cloves
- ✓ 2 tablespoons tahini
- ✓ 2 tablespoons olive oil

- ✓ Juice of 1 lemon
- ✓ Salt to taste
- ✓ Variety of sliced veggies (carrots, cucumbers, bell peppers, etc.)

Step-by-Step Preparation:

1. Drain and rinse the chickpeas.
2. Combine chickpeas, garlic, tahini, olive oil, lemon juice, and salt in a blender or food processor. Blend until smooth.
3. Adjust seasoning to taste.
4. Serve hummus dip with a variety of sliced vegetables.

Nutritional Facts: (Per serving)

- ❖ Calories: 150
- ❖ Protein: 6g
- ❖ Carbs: 14g
- ❖ Fat: 9g
- ❖ Fiber: 4g

End your day with this balanced, nutrient-dense snack. This simple, vegan-friendly recipe combines the creaminess of hummus with the fresh crunch of veggies, helping satisfy late-night cravings without hindering your weight loss journey. Keep the ingredients on hand for a healthy treat anytime.

Recipe 59: Bowl of Oatmeal Porridge With Blueberries

Indulge in a healthy midnight snack with this Bowl of Oatmeal Porridge with Blueberries and Almond Nuts. This high-protein, low-fat dish can satisfy your late-night cravings while assisting in your weight loss goals.

Servings: 1

Prepping Time: 10 minutes

Cook Time: 10 minutes

Difficulty: Easy

Ingredients:

- ✓ 1/2 cup of rolled oats
- ✓ 1 cup of almond milk
- ✓ A handful of fresh blueberries
- ✓ 10 almond nuts, chopped
- ✓ Sweetener of choice (optional)

✓ A dash of cinnamon (optional)

Step-by-Step Preparation:

1. In a pot, bring the almond milk to a boil.

2. Add the oats to the boiling milk, reduce the heat, and let it simmer.

3. Stir occasionally for about 10 minutes until the oats are creamy.

4. Once cooked, transfer the oatmeal into a bowl.

5. Top it off with fresh blueberries, chopped almonds, and your choice of sweetener and cinnamon.

Nutritional Facts: (Per serving)

❖ Calories: 300 kcal

❖ Protein: 12 g

❖ Fat: 10 g

❖ Carbohydrates: 40 g

❖ Fiber: 9 g

❖ Sugar: 10 g

This comforting bowl of Oatmeal Porridge with Blueberries and Almond Nuts nourishes your body and aids your weight loss journey. It's the perfect balance of heartiness and sweetness for those late-night snack cravings.

Recipe 60: Homemade Green Kale Chips With Vegan Cheese

Welcome to a delightful, guilt-free snack bursting with flavors and nutrients! Homemade Green Kale Chips with Vegan Cheese, a perfect midnight munch, satisfy your taste buds and aid in weight loss with high protein content.

Servings: 4

Prepping Time: 10 minutes

Cook Time: 15 minutes

Difficulty: Easy

Ingredients:

- ✓ 1 large bunch of kale
- ✓ 1 tablespoon olive oil
- ✓ 2 tablespoons nutritional yeast
- ✓ 1/4 cup vegan cheese

✓   Salt to taste

Step-by-Step Preparation:

1. Preheat your oven to 300°F (150°C) and line a baking sheet with parchment paper.

2. Wash and thoroughly dry the kale, then tear it into bite-sized pieces.

3. Drizzle kale with olive oil and sprinkle with nutritional yeast, vegan cheese, and salt.

4. Arrange the kale pieces on the prepared baking sheet and bake for 10-15 minutes until crisp.

5. Let the kale chips cool before serving.

Nutritional Facts: (Per serving)

❖   Calories: 80

❖   Protein: 6g

❖   Carbohydrates: 10g

❖   Fat: 2g

❖   Fiber: 2g

Savor these delectable Homemade Green Kale Chips with Vegan Cheese, a snacking heaven that treats your palate while giving a powerful punch of nutrients. High in protein and low in calories, this delightful snack fuels your late-night cravings without worrying about your weight loss journey.

Chapter 07: Protein-Rich Seafood Dishes

Recipe 61: Shrimp and Zucchini Noodles

Unleash the flavors of the ocean and the garden with this delightful Shrimp and Zucchini Noodles pasta. This high-protein, low-carb dish is a perfect partner for your weight loss journey, blending succulent shrimp with zesty chili and parmesan-encrusted zoodles cooked to perfection in a cast-iron pan.

Servings: 4

Prepping Time: 15 minutes

Cook Time: 20 minutes

Difficulty: Easy

Ingredients:

- ✓ 1 lb peeled and deveined Shrimp
- ✓ 4 medium Zucchinis, spiralized into zoodles

- ✓ 2 tbsp Olive Oil
- ✓ 4 cloves Garlic, minced
- ✓ 1 tsp Red Chili Flakes
- ✓ 1/2 cup Grated Parmesan Cheese
- ✓ Salt and Pepper to taste
- ✓ Fresh Parsley for garnish

Step-by-Step Preparation:

1. In a large cast-iron pan, heat the olive oil over medium heat. Add the garlic and chili flakes, and saute until fragrant.

2. Add the shrimp to the pan, season with salt and Pepper. Cook until the shrimp turn pink, then remove and set aside.

3. In the same pan, add the zoodles and cook for 2-3 minutes until they are tender but still have a crunch.

4. Return the shrimp to the pan, add the parmesan cheese, and toss until everything is well-coated.

5. Serve hot, garnished with fresh parsley.

Nutritional Facts: (Per serving)

- ❖ Calories: 280
- ❖ Protein: 30g
- ❖ Fat: 10g
- ❖ Carbohydrates: 10g
- ❖ Fiber: 3g
- ❖ Sugar: 6g

Reinvigorate your diet plan with this delicious Shrimp and Zucchini Noodles dish. Not only does it pack a flavorful punch, but it also offers a rich source of protein to aid in your weight loss journey. It's a simple, guilt-free way to enjoy pasta. Here's to healthy eating without sacrificing taste!

Recipe 62: Black Beans & Quinoa Seafood Pasta

Discover the perfect blend of health and taste with this Black Beans & Quinoa Seafood Pasta, a high-protein dish that pairs the rich flavors of seared scallops and mixed seafood with hearty black beans and nutritious quinoa. Tossed in an olive oil white wine sauce with garlic, tomatoes, onions, shredded parmesan, and green onions, it's the perfect meal for weight loss.

Servings: 4

Prepping Time: 20 minutes

Cook Time: 30 minutes

Difficulty: Medium

Ingredients:

- ✓ 1 cup quinoa and 2 cups black beans
- ✓ 1 lb mixed seafood and 1 lb scallops
- ✓ 1/2 cup olive oil and 1/2 cup white wine
- ✓ 4 cloves garlic and 2 medium tomatoes

- ✓ 1 large onion
- ✓ 1/2 cup shredded parmesan cheese
- ✓ 2 green onions

Step-by-Step Preparation:

1. Cook quinoa and black beans as per package instructions.
2. Sear scallops and seafood in a hot pan with some olive oil.
3. Saute garlic, tomatoes, and onions in olive oil until softened.
4. Add white wine and let it simmer.
5. Toss in cooked quinoa, black beans, seared seafood, and parmesan cheese. Mix well.
6. Garnish with green onions before serving.

Nutritional Facts: (Per serving)

- ❖ Calories: 500
- ❖ Protein: 35g
- ❖ Carbs: 45g
- ❖ Fat: 20g
- ❖ Fiber: 15g
- ❖ Sodium: 550mg

Finish your day on a high note with this delicious, protein-packed Black Beans & Quinoa Seafood Pasta. It's a weight loss-friendly recipe that doesn't skimp on flavor or nutrition, providing you with the energy you need while helping you stay on track with your fitness goals. So go ahead, and make your taste buds and waistline happy with this delicious seafood dish.

Recipe 63: Raw Organic Ahi Tuna Poke Bowl With Rice and Veggies

Embrace the tropical island flavors with this Raw Organic Ahi Tuna Poke Bowl. Fresh, nutritious, and bursting with umami, this traditional Hawaiian dish fuses raw seafood with veggies and rice, making a high-protein meal perfect for weight loss.

Servings: 4

Prepping Time: 20 minutes

Cook Time: 30 minutes

Difficulty: Medium

Ingredients:

- ✓ 500g Raw organic ahi tuna
- ✓ 2 cups Sushi rice
- ✓ 1 Avocado
- ✓ 1 Cucumber

- ✓ 1 cup Shredded carrots
- ✓ 4 tbsp Soy sauce
- ✓ 2 tsp Sesame oil
- ✓ 1 tbsp Honey
- ✓ 2 Green onions
- ✓ 1 tsp Sesame seeds

Step-by-Step Preparation:

1. Cook the sushi rice according to the package instructions.
2. Dice the ahi tuna and chop the avocado, cucumber, and green onions.
3. Combine the soy sauce, sesame oil, and honey in a bowl to create a marinade.
4. Add the diced tuna to the marinade and refrigerate for 15 minutes.
5. Assemble the bowl with rice, marinated tuna, and veggies. Sprinkle with sesame seeds and serve immediately.

Nutritional Facts: (Per serving)

- ❖ Calories: 540 kcal
- ❖ Protein: 40g
- ❖ Carbohydrates: 55g
- ❖ Fat: 15g
- ❖ Fiber: 6g
- ❖ Sugar: 6g

Relish the vibrant and delightful Raw Organic Ahi Tuna Poke Bowl, a harmony of taste and health. Its high protein content and wide array of nutrients promote weight loss while satisfying your cravings for a flavorful seafood dish. Dive into this nutritious recipe and relish the aloha spirit in every bite!

Recipe 64: Homemade Grilled Salmon With Dill

This Homemade Grilled Salmon with Dill recipe offers a flavorful and nutritious meal. It's high in protein, making it perfect for weight loss, and it carries the fresh taste of the sea in every bite.

Servings: 4

Prepping Time: 15 minutes

Cook Time: 15 minutes

Difficulty: Easy

Ingredients:

- ✓ 4 salmon fillets (6 ounces each)
- ✓ 1 tablespoon olive oil
- ✓ Salt and pepper to taste
- ✓ 1 tablespoon fresh dill, chopped
- ✓ 1 lemon, sliced

Step-by-Step Preparation:

1. Preheat your grill to medium heat.

2. Rub the salmon fillets with olive oil, salt, and pepper.

3. Place the salmon on the grill, skin side down.

4. Grill for 6-8 minutes per side or until salmon is cooked to your liking.

5. Sprinkle the fresh dill and squeeze the lemon juice over the cooked salmon before serving.

Nutritional Facts: (Per serving)

- ❖ Calories: 367

- ❖ Protein: 39g

- ❖ Carbs: 0g

- ❖ Fat: 22g

- ❖ Fiber: 0g

- ❖ Sodium: 98mg

Celebrate the exquisite flavor of the sea with this Homemade Grilled Salmon with Dill recipe. High in protein, low in carbs, and delightful in taste, this dish is your go-to choice for a healthy, weight-loss-friendly, and utterly satisfying meal.

Recipe 65: Mussels With French Fries and White Wine

Discover a taste of the sea with this exquisite Mussels with French Fries and White Wine recipe, an irresistible combination of succulent mussels, crispy fries, and a tangy white wine sauce. High in protein, this seafood delight is perfect for a weight loss diet, satisfying your taste buds while keeping your waistline in check.

Servings: 4

Prepping Time: 15 minutes

Cook Time: 20 minutes

Difficulty: Medium

Ingredients:

- ✓ 2 pounds of fresh mussels, cleaned
- ✓ 2 large russet potatoes, cut into fries
- ✓ 2 tablespoons olive oil
- ✓ 1 cup dry white wine

✓ 2 shallots, finely chopped

✓ 4 cloves of garlic, minced

✓ 1/4 cup chopped fresh parsley

✓ Salt and pepper to taste

Step-by-Step Preparation:

1. Preheat your oven to 425°F (220°C). Toss fries in olive oil, spread on a baking sheet, season with salt, and bake until crispy, about 20 minutes.

2. Meanwhile, sauté shallots and garlic in a large pan until soft. Add white wine and bring to a simmer.

3. Add mussels, cover the pan, and steam until they open up, about 5-7 minutes. Discard any mussels that do not open.

4. Serve mussels with the white wine sauce, garnished with fresh parsley, and a side of crispy French fries.

Nutritional Facts: (Per serving)

❖ Calories: 350

❖ Protein: 28g

❖ Fat: 10g

❖ Carbs: 35g

❖ Fiber: 2g

Dive into this delicious and health-conscious Mussels with French Fries and White Wine recipe! Perfect for a casual dinner or an elegant get-together, this dish allows you to indulge in a meal that not only satiates your cravings but also contributes to your weight loss journey. Enjoy this combination of flavors and textures, a true testament to the joys of seafood cuisine.

Recipe 66: Pan Fried Cod Loin With Courgettes

Take your tastebuds on a flavorful journey with this high-protein seafood dish. This pan-fried cod loin recipe, complemented by courgettes, tomatoes, basil, parmesan, and pumpkin seeds, brings the fresh flavors of pesto to your dinner table, all while aiding your weight loss efforts.

Servings: 4

Prepping Time: 20 minutes

Cook Time: 15 minutes

Difficulty: Medium

Ingredients:

- ✓ 4 Cod loins
- ✓ 2 Courgettes, thinly sliced
- ✓ 2 Tomatoes, chopped
- ✓ 1 Handful of fresh basil leaves

- ✓ 50g Grated parmesan
- ✓ 30g Pumpkin seeds
- ✓ Olive oil, salt, and pepper for seasoning

Step-by-Step Preparation:

1. Preheat your pan, drizzle olive oil, then add the cod loins. Cook for about 7 minutes on each side until golden brown. Remove and set aside.

2. Add the courgettes and tomatoes to the same pan, and cook until softened.

3. Return the cod to the pan, add the basil, parmesan, and pumpkin seeds. Stir gently to combine.

4. Season with salt and pepper. Let it simmer for a few minutes for the flavors to infuse.

5. Serve hot, garnished with more basil if desired.

Nutritional Facts: (Per serving)

- ❖ Calories: 310
- ❖ Protein: 40g
- ❖ Fat: 14g
- ❖ Carbohydrates: 7g
- ❖ Fiber: 2g
- ❖ Sodium: 420mg

Relish in the juiciness of pan-fried cod loin, elevated by an array of pesto-inspired flavors. A deliciously healthy meal that doesn't compromise on taste, providing you with a protein-packed, weight-loss-friendly dish. The perfect combination of health and pleasure in every bite. Enjoy this culinary delight as part of your diet, and witness the transformative power of nutritious eating.

Recipe 67: Baked Cajun Catfish With French Fries

Unearth the flavors of the bayou with our Spicy Homemade Baked Cajun Catfish accompanied by crispy French fries. This high-protein seafood dish is a weight-loss-friendly meal with spices and savory goodness, perfect for weeknight dinners or special occasions.

Servings: 4

Prepping Time: 15 minutes

Cook Time: 30 minutes

Difficulty: Medium

Ingredients:

- ✓   4 catfish fillets (around 6 ounces each)
- ✓   2 tablespoons Cajun seasoning
- ✓   1 teaspoon garlic powder
- ✓   1 teaspoon onion powder

- ✓ 2 large russet potatoes, cut into fries
- ✓ 2 tablespoons olive oil
- ✓ Salt and pepper to taste

Step-by-Step Preparation:

1. Preheat your oven to 425°F (220°C) and line a baking sheet with parchment paper.

2. Mix the Cajun seasoning, garlic powder, and onion powder in a small bowl.

3. Pat the catfish dry and rub the spice mixture on both sides of each fillet.

4. Toss the cut potatoes in olive oil, salt, and pepper, then spread out on a baking sheet.

5. Bake the catfish and fries in the oven for 15-20 minutes, or until the fish is opaque and flakes easily and the fries are golden and crisp.

Nutritional Facts: (Per serving)

- ❖ Calories: 380
- ❖ Protein: 30g
- ❖ Carbohydrates: 25g
- ❖ Dietary Fiber: 3g
- ❖ Fat: 18g
- ❖ Sodium: 650mg

Make your dinner nights unforgettable with this Spicy Homemade Baked Cajun Catfish with French fries. It's a simple yet delicious seafood recipe that doesn't compromise on taste while helping you achieve your weight loss goals. Enjoy the culinary journey to the bayou right in your kitchen!

Recipe 68: Grilled Tuna Steak Slices With Mango Salsa

Indulge in a high-protein meal that's both nutritious and flavorsome. Grilled tuna steak slices are served alongside vibrant mango salsa and a refreshing vegetable salad for a balanced meal. This recipe is designed with weight loss in mind without compromising on taste.

Servings: 4

Prepping Time: 25 minutes

Cook Time: 10 minutes

Difficulty: Moderate

Ingredients:

- ✓ 4 Tuna Steaks
- ✓ 2 ripe Mangoes
- ✓ 1 Red Onion
- ✓ 2 Jalapeno Peppers

- ✓ 1 bunch of Cilantro
- ✓ 2 Lemons
- ✓ Salt and Pepper to taste
- ✓ Olive Oil
- ✓ 1 Bell Pepper
- ✓ Mixed Salad Greens

Step-by-Step Preparation:

1. Preheat the grill and season tuna steaks with salt, Pepper, and olive oil.

2. Grill each side of the tuna steaks for 3-4 minutes.

3. Dice mangoes, onion, jalapeno peppers, bell pepper, and cilantro, combine them in a bowl, add lemon juice, and season with salt and Pepper to make the salsa.

4. Toss the mixed salad greens in olive oil and lemon juice.

5. Serve the grilled tuna with the mango salsa and salad on the side.

Nutritional Facts: (Per serving)

- ❖ Calories: 400 kcal
- ❖ Protein: 40g
- ❖ Carbohydrates: 20g
- ❖ Fat: 15g
- ❖ Fiber: 5g
- ❖ Sugars: 10g

Enjoy this fulfilling, high-protein meal that satisfies your seafood cravings while aiding your weight loss journey. Grilled tuna steak slices with mango salsa and vegetable salad are a feast for the eyes and an explosion of flavors and nutrients in every bite.

Recipe 69: Fried Shrimp and Asparagus With Mushrooms

A delightful fusion of seafood and vegetables, this Fried Shrimp and Asparagus with Mushrooms dish is your ideal high-protein meal for weight loss. Combining the tender shrimp with the crunch of asparagus and the earthiness of the mushroom's nutritious delicacy will satisfy your palate.

Servings: 4

Prepping Time: 15 Minutes

Cook Time: 15 Minutes

Difficulty: Easy

Ingredients:

- ✓ 500g Fresh Shrimp, peeled and deveined
- ✓ 2 Bunches of Asparagus, trimmed and cut into 2-inch pieces
- ✓ 200g Mixed Mushrooms, sliced
- ✓ 3 Cloves Garlic, minced

- ✓ 2 Tbsp Olive Oil

- ✓ Salt and Pepper to taste

- ✓ Lemon Wedges for serving

Step-by-Step Preparation:

1. Heat oil in a pan over medium heat.

2. Add garlic and sauté until fragrant.

3. Add shrimp and cook until they turn pink, around 2-3 minutes. Remove and set aside.

4. In the same pan, add asparagus and mushrooms. Sauté until tender.

5. Return the shrimp to the pan, season with salt and Pepper. Stir everything together.

6. Serve with a squeeze of fresh lemon.

Nutritional Facts: (Per serving)

- ❖ Calories: 220

- ❖ Protein: 25g

- ❖ Fat: 9g

- ❖ Carbs: 10g

- ❖ Fiber: 3g

- ❖ Sugars: 2g

Round off your day with this delectable Fried Shrimp and Asparagus with Mushrooms dish as you enjoy its flavors and health benefits. Easy to prepare, it's a go-to meal for a healthy weight loss journey while keeping your taste buds entertained.

Recipe 70: Cucumber Rolls With Salmon

Indulge in a refreshing bite with these cucumber rolls, packed with heart-healthy salmon, creamy cheese, and zesty lemon. Perfect for weight loss, they're high in protein and irresistibly tasty.

Servings: 4

Prepping Time: 20 minutes

Cook Time: 0 minutes

Difficulty: Easy

Ingredients:

- ✓ 2 large cucumbers
- ✓ 8 oz smoked salmon
- ✓ 4 oz cream cheese
- ✓ 1 lemon, zest, and juice
- ✓ Fresh dill for garnish
- ✓ Salt and pepper to taste

Step-by-Step Preparation:

1. Peel and slice cucumbers lengthwise into thin strips using a vegetable peeler.

2. Spread a thin layer of cream cheese over each cucumber strip.

3. Layer smoked salmon slices over the cream cheese.

4. Sprinkle with lemon zest, a squeeze of lemon juice, salt, and pepper.

5. Roll up the cucumber strips and secure them with a toothpick.

6. Garnish with fresh dill before serving.

Nutritional Facts: (Per serving)

- ❖ Calories: 180
- ❖ Protein: 15g
- ❖ Fat: 10g
- ❖ Carbohydrates: 6g
- ❖ Fiber: 1g

Elevate your seafood meals with these delightful cucumber rolls with salmon, cream cheese, and lemon. This high-protein, low-carb recipe is your ultimate aid in weight loss without sacrificing flavor and satisfaction. Enjoy a roll or two for a light meal, appetizer, or snack!

Chapter 08: Protein Smoothies and Drinks

Recipe 71: Chocolate Protein Shake With Almond Milk

Prepare your taste buds for a deliciously healthy, homemade Chocolate Protein Shake. Made with almond milk and a punch of protein shake is perfect for weight loss and can be easily prepared as a refreshing drink or a post-workout smoothie.

Servings: 2

Prepping Time: 5 minutes

Cook Time: 0 minutes

Difficulty: Easy

Ingredients:

- ✓ 2 cups unsweetened almond milk

- ✓ 2 scoops chocolate protein powder

- ✓ 1 ripe banana
- ✓ 1 tbsp unsweetened cocoa powder
- ✓ 1 tbsp honey (optional)
- ✓ A handful of ice cubes

Step-by-Step Preparation:

1. Place all ingredients in a blender.
2. Blend until smooth and creamy.
3. Pour the shake into two glasses and serve immediately.

Nutritional Facts: (Per serving)

- ❖ Calories: 240
- ❖ Protein: 26g
- ❖ Fat: 4g
- ❖ Carbs: 30g
- ❖ Sugars: 10g
- ❖ Fiber: 5g

Relish this healthy Chocolate Protein Shake to keep you full and satisfied. Whether trying to lose weight or just seeking a delicious, protein-packed snack, this shake will not disappoint. Enjoy its creamy texture and chocolatey goodness anytime, anywhere. Stay fit, stay healthy!

Recipe 72: Colorful Vegan Smoothies

Kick off your day with these high-protein vegan smoothies. Two delightful options - Blackberry Banana Oatmeal Smoothie and Kiwi Spinach Smoothie - are colorful, tasty, and packed with nutrition. They are perfect for a quick breakfast, snack, or weight loss.

Servings: 2

Prepping Time: 10 Minutes

Cook Time: 0 Minutes

Difficulty: Easy

Ingredients:

- ✓ 1 ripe banana
- ✓ 1/2 cup blackberries
- ✓ 1/2 cup oatmeal
- ✓ 2 kiwis
- ✓ 1 cup spinach

- ✓ 2 cups almond milk

- ✓ 2 tablespoons chia seeds

- ✓ 2 tablespoons protein powder

Step-by-Step Preparation:

1. For the Blackberry Banana Oatmeal Smoothie: Blend banana, blackberries, 1 cup almond milk, 1 tablespoon chia seeds, 1 tablespoon protein powder, and oatmeal until smooth.

2. For the Kiwi Spinach Smoothie: Blend kiwis, spinach, remaining 1 cup almond milk, 1 tablespoon chia seeds, and 1 tablespoon protein powder until smooth.

Nutritional Facts: (Per serving)

- ❖ Calories: 265

- ❖ Protein: 15g

- ❖ Fiber: 9g

- ❖ Fat: 8g

- ❖ Carbohydrates: 34g

These simple and nutritious vegan smoothies are your best allies when losing weight or maintaining a healthy lifestyle. Not only do they promote satiety, but they also provide a substantial amount of fiber and protein, essential for your body's needs. Enjoy them in the morning or as a mid-day snack for a refreshing, healthful boost.

Recipe 73: Vanilla Banana Smoothie

Embrace a delicious fusion of flavors with our High Protein Vanilla Banana Smoothie, enriched with cookies and chocolate. It's a healthy, delectable delight that doesn't compromise on taste while helping you lose weight!

Servings: 2

Prepping Time: 10 minutes

Cook Time: 0 minutes

Difficulty: Easy

Ingredients:

- ✓ 2 ripe bananas
- ✓ 2 cups of almond milk
- ✓ 1 scoop of vanilla protein powder
- ✓ 2 tablespoons of honey
- ✓ 1/4 cup of dark chocolate chips
- ✓ 2 cookies, crushed

Step-by-Step Preparation:

1. Peel and slice the bananas, then freeze them for 2 hours.

2. Place the frozen bananas in a blender.

3. Add almond milk, protein powder, and honey, and blend until smooth.

4. Stir in crushed cookies and chocolate chips.

5. Pour the smoothie into glasses and serve immediately.

Nutritional Facts: (Per serving)

❖ Calories: 300

❖ Protein: 15g

❖ Carbohydrates: 50g

❖ Fat: 7g

❖ Fiber: 5g

❖ Sugar: 25g

Indulge in this delightful High Protein Vanilla Banana Smoothie with cookies and chocolate, a perfect combo of taste and health. This smoothie is a quick, easy, and delicious way to boost your protein intake while losing weight. Make it a part of your daily diet and feel the difference!

Recipe 74: Fruit Mango Yogurt With Fresh Mint

Delve into the tropical delight of Fruit Mango Yogurt with Fresh Mint - a high protein, weight loss-friendly smoothie that's vibrant, refreshing, and easy to prepare.

Servings: 2

Prepping Time: 10 minutes

Cook Time: 0 minutes

Difficulty: Easy

Ingredients:

- ✓ 1 large ripe mango, peeled and diced
- ✓ 1 cup low-fat Greek yogurt
- ✓ A handful of fresh mint leaves
- ✓ 1 tablespoon honey or to taste
- ✓ 1/2 cup of ice cubes

Step-by-Step Preparation:

1. Combine the mango, Greek yogurt, fresh mint, and honey in a blender.

2. Blend until smooth, add the ice cubes, and blend until creamy.

3. Pour the smoothie into two glasses and garnish with a sprig of mint.

Nutritional Facts: (Per serving)

❖ Calories: 150

❖ Protein: 10 grams

❖ Carbohydrates: 20 grams

❖ Fat: 2 grams

❖ Fiber: 3 grams

Sip on this energizing and health-boosting Fruit Mango Yogurt with Fresh Mint smoothie, a perfect blend of nutrition and taste. The creamy texture, paired with the tartness of the mango and cool mint, makes for a delightful drink that promotes weight loss and satisfies cravings.

Recipe 75: A Green Organic Drink

Delve into a healthier lifestyle with this nourishing organic green drink. The weight-loss-promoting beverage is a powerhouse of nutrients. It's an energizing way to kickstart your day and support your fitness goals.

Servings: 2

Prepping Time: 10 minutes

Cook Time: 0 minutes

Difficulty: Easy

Ingredients:

- ✓ 2 cups raw spinach
- ✓ 1 medium cucumber
- ✓ 1 green apple
- ✓ 1/2 medium avocado
- ✓ 1 tablespoon chia seeds
- ✓ 2 scoops protein powder (optional)

✓ 1.5 cups unsweetened almond milk

Step-by-Step Preparation:

1. Wash and chop the vegetables.

2. Put all ingredients into a blender.

3. Blend until smooth and creamy.

4. Pour the drink into glasses and serve immediately.

Nutritional Facts: (Per serving)

❖ Calories: 230

❖ Protein: 15g

❖ Fiber: 8g

❖ Fat: 10g

❖ Carbs: 20g

❖ Sugars: 10g

Indulge in the freshness and refreshing flavor of this organic green drink. It's not just a weight loss smoothie. It's a commitment to your health. Enjoy it in the morning for a refreshing start or as a post-workout treat to replenish your body. The perfect blend of tasty and healthy awaits you!

Recipe 76: Healthy Detox Vitamin Diet Colorful Smoothie

Unleash the power of nutrition with this vibrant, health-boosting smoothie. The high-protein delight bursting with spinach, pomegranate, figs, and blueberries is perfect for those seeking a delicious weight-loss tool or an energizing breakfast.

Servings: 2

Prepping Time: 10 minutes

Cook Time: 0 minutes

Difficulty: Easy

Ingredients:

- ✓ 1 cup fresh spinach
- ✓ Seeds from 1 pomegranate
- ✓ 2 fresh figs
- ✓ 1/2 cup fresh blueberries

- ✓ 1 scoop of protein powder
- ✓ 1 cup almond milk
- ✓ Ice (optional)

Step-by-Step Preparation:

1. Wash all the fruits thoroughly.

2. Deseed the pomegranate, and cut the figs into quarters.

3. Combine spinach, pomegranate seeds, figs, blueberries, protein powder, and almond milk in a blender.

4. Blend until smooth. If preferred colder, add ice and blend again.

5. Pour into glasses and serve immediately.

Nutritional Facts: (Per serving)

- ❖ Calories: 200
- ❖ Protein: 20g
- ❖ Carbs: 25g
- ❖ Fiber: 5g
- ❖ Sugars: 15g
- ❖ Fat: 4g

Relish this nutritious, protein-packed smoothie that's as delightful to the taste buds as it is to the eyes. With its rich flavors and healthful ingredients, it's not just a drink but a lifestyle choice for weight loss, wellness, and a brighter day.

Recipe 77: Healthy Coffee Banana Oat Smoothie

Embrace a nourishing kickstart to your day with a Healthy Coffee Banana Oat Smoothie. This high-protein, low-fat blend offers the dual advantage of tantalizing taste and weight management, keeping you filled and energized throughout the day.

Servings: 2

Prepping Time: 5 minutes

Cook Time: 0 minutes

Difficulty: Easy

Ingredients:

- ✓ 1 ripe banana
- ✓ 1 cup brewed coffee, chilled
- ✓ 1/2 cup rolled oats
- ✓ 1 cup unsweetened almond milk

- ✓ 1 scoop protein powder

- ✓ 1 tablespoon honey or agave nectar (optional)

- ✓ Ice cubes

Step-by-Step Preparation:

1. Combine banana, chilled coffee, oats, almond milk, protein powder, sweetener (if using), and ice cubes in a blender.

2. Blend until smooth and creamy.

3. Pour into glasses and serve immediately.

Nutritional Facts: (Per serving)

- ❖ Calories: 220

- ❖ Protein: 16g

- ❖ Carbs: 34g

- ❖ Fat: 3g

- ❖ Fiber: 4g

- ❖ Sugar: 14g

Jumpstart your weight loss journey with this easy, nutritious, delicious Coffee Banana Oat Smoothie. Not only does it satiate your morning hunger and caffeine cravings, it also acts as a catalyst in achieving your health and wellness goals. A delightful drink that's easy to make and easier to enjoy!

Recipe 78: Healthy Pineapple Smoothie

Kick-start your weight loss journey with a Healthy Pineapple Smoothie. Bursting with natural sweetness and packed with protein, this vibrant tropical drink is the perfect fuel for your fitness regimen and provides a refreshing twist on a classic healthy drink.

Servings: 2

Prepping Time: 5 Minutes

Cook Time: No Cook Time Required

Difficulty: Easy

Ingredients:

- ✓ 1 cup frozen pineapple

- ✓ 1 medium ripe banana

- ✓ 1 cup unsweetened almond milk

- ✓ 1 scoop vanilla protein powder

- ✓ 1 tbsp chia seeds

✓ Ice cubes (optional)

Step-by-Step Preparation:

1. Gather all your ingredients.

2. In a blender, combine the frozen pineapple, ripe banana, almond milk, and protein powder.

3. Blend until smooth.

4. Add the chia seeds and blend again for a few seconds.

5. If desired, add ice cubes for a colder smoothie and blend until ice is crushed.

6. Serve immediately and enjoy your refreshing high protein smoothie!

Nutritional Facts: (Per serving)

❖ Calories: 220

❖ Protein: 18g

❖ Carbohydrates: 36g

❖ Fat: 3g

❖ Fiber: 6g

❖ Sugar: 23g

Incorporating this Healthy Pineapple Smoothie into your weight loss plan will offer a delightful treat without derailing your diet. This high protein smoothie is both satisfying and nourishing, making it an ideal choice for those looking to maintain a balanced, nutrient-rich diet while enjoying the vibrant flavors of a tropical getaway.

Recipe 79: Iced Coffee Protein Shake

Kick-start your day with a refreshing and healthy Iced Coffee Protein Shake. The protein-packed smoothie satisfies your caffeine cravings and keeps you full, making dieting enjoyable.

Servings: 2

Prepping Time: 10 minutes

Cook Time: 0 minutes

Difficulty: Easy

Ingredients:

- ✓ 2 cups cold brewed coffee
- ✓ 1 ripe banana
- ✓ 2 scoops of protein powder (chocolate or vanilla)
- ✓ 1 cup unsweetened almond milk
- ✓ 2 cups of ice cubes
- ✓ Optional: sweetener to taste

Step-by-Step Preparation:

1. Combine the coffee, banana, protein powder, and almond milk in a blender.

2. Add ice cubes and blend until smooth.

3. If desired, add sweetener and blend again until mixed.

4. Pour into glasses and serve immediately.

Nutritional Facts: (Per serving)

❖ Calories: 180 kcal

❖ Protein: 25g

❖ Carbohydrates: 20g

❖ Fat: 3g

❖ Fiber: 3g

❖ Sugar: 8g

Close your morning with this nutrient-dense Iced Coffee Protein Shake and say goodbye to bland weight loss meals. With the combination of taste and health, this shake helps you lose weight and boosts your energy levels, preparing you for the day ahead.

Recipe 80: Green Smoothie

Dive into a refreshing world of health with this detox green smoothie packed with protein and ideal for weight loss. This smoothie is delicious, nutritious, and the perfect start to your day or post-workout refresher.

Servings: 2

Prepping Time: 5 minutes

Cook Time: No cooking required

Difficulty: Easy

Ingredients:

- ✓ 1 cup of spinach
- ✓ 1 ripe banana
- ✓ 1 cup of almond milk
- ✓ 2 tablespoons of protein powder
- ✓ 1 tablespoon of honey
- ✓ A handful of ice cubes

Step-by-Step Preparation:

1. Place all the ingredients into a blender.

2. Blend until the mixture is smooth and creamy.

3. Pour into glasses and serve immediately.

Nutritional Facts: (Per serving)

- ❖ Calories: 160 kcal

- ❖ Protein: 8 g

- ❖ Carbs: 27 g

- ❖ Fiber: 3 g

- ❖ Fat: 3 g

Ending your day with this green detox smoothie can be a game-changer. Its ingredients will cleanse your system, and its high protein content aids in muscle recovery and weight loss. Say yes to a healthy lifestyle with this simple, delicious, and easy-to-make smoothie!

Chapter 09: Protein-Infused Salads

Recipe 81: Greek Salad With Grilled Chicken

Embark on a Mediterranean culinary adventure with this Greek Salad with Grilled Chicken. A delicious blend of tangy flavors and wholesome ingredients, it's perfect for weight loss due to its high protein content and low calories.

Servings: 4

Prepping Time: 20 minutes

Cook Time: 15 minutes

Difficulty: Easy

Ingredients:

- ✓ 2 large boneless chicken breasts
- ✓ 1 large cucumber
- ✓ 2 large ripe tomatoes

- ✓ 1 red onion

- ✓ 1 cup Kalamata olives

- ✓ 1/2 cup feta cheese

- ✓ 4 cups Romaine lettuce

- ✓ 1 lemon

- ✓ Olive oil, salt, pepper, oregano for dressing

Step-by-Step Preparation:

1. Marinate chicken with olive oil, salt, pepper, and oregano. Grill until fully cooked.

2. Chop cucumber, tomatoes, red onion, and Romaine lettuce. Toss in a bowl.

3. Add olives and crumbled feta cheese.

4. Slice grilled chicken and add to the salad.

5. Add olive oil, lemon juice, and seasoning to make the dressing. Drizzle over salad before serving.

Nutritional Facts: (Per serving)

- ❖ Calories: 350

- ❖ Protein: 30g

- ❖ Fat: 15g

- ❖ Carbohydrates: 15g

- ❖ Fiber: 4g

- ❖ Sodium: 500mg

End your day with this Greek Salad with Grilled Chicken, an exemplary fusion of taste and nutrition. Offering a refreshing twist to your daily meal recipe is your ultimate companion for weight loss, providing ample protein without compromising on flavor.

Recipe 82: Quinoa Salad, Vegetarian Food

Indulge in this scrumptiously satisfying Quinoa Salad, a vegetarian delight with abundant flavors. This high-protein meal is ideal for weight loss while keeping your taste buds tickled.

Servings: 4

Prepping Time: 15 minutes

Cook Time: 15 minutes

Difficulty: Easy

Ingredients:

- ✓ 1 cup quinoa
- ✓ 2 cups water
- ✓ 1 cup chopped bell peppers
- ✓ 1 cup cherry tomatoes, halved
- ✓ 1 cup cucumber, diced
- ✓ 1/2 cup red onion, diced

- ✓ 1/2 cup chopped parsley
- ✓ Juice of one lemon
- ✓ 2 tablespoons extra virgin olive oil
- ✓ Salt and pepper to taste

Step-by-Step Preparation:

1. Rinse the quinoa under cold water until the water runs clear.

2. Boil quinoa in the water and simmer for 15 minutes or until tender.

3. Combine cooked quinoa, bell peppers, cherry tomatoes, cucumber, and red onion in a large bowl.

4. Whisk together lemon juice, olive oil, salt, and pepper in a small bowl.

5. Pour the dressing over the salad and toss until well mixed. Add parsley and give a final toss.

Nutritional Facts: (Per serving)

- ❖ Calories: 220
- ❖ Protein: 8g
- ❖ Fat: 7g
- ❖ Carbohydrates: 32g
- ❖ Fiber: 5g
- ❖ Sugar: 4g

Dive into this Quinoa Salad, a harmony of crisp vegetables and wholesome quinoa drizzled with zesty lemon dressing. A perfect choice for a light lunch or a side dish that leaves you satisfied without the guilt. Enjoy this tasty, health-packed recipe that fits into any weight loss plan.

Recipe 83: Cucumber Tuna Avocado Salad

Savor a delicious fusion of health and flavor with the Cucumber Tuna Avocado Salad, a refreshing mix of crunchy cucumbers, creamy avocado, and protein-rich tuna. This high-protein meal is ideal for weight loss, offering nutrition and taste in every bite.

Servings: 4

Prepping Time: 15 minutes

Cook Time: 0 minutes

Difficulty: Easy

Ingredients:

- ✓ 2 medium cucumbers, sliced
- ✓ 2 ripe avocados, diced
- ✓ 1 can of tuna, drained
- ✓ 1 red onion, finely chopped
- ✓ 2 tbsp olive oil

- ✓ 1 lemon, juiced
- ✓ Salt and pepper to taste

Step-by-Step Preparation:

1. Combine cucumbers, avocado, tuna, and red onion in a large bowl.

2. Whisk together the olive oil, lemon juice, salt, and pepper in a separate bowl.

3. Pour the dressing over the salad and toss until everything is well coated.

4. Refrigerate for 30 minutes before serving.

Nutritional Facts: (Per serving)

- ❖ Calories: 210
- ❖ Protein: 18g
- ❖ Carbs: 9g
- ❖ Fat: 13g
- ❖ Fiber: 5g
- ❖ Sugar: 2g

Revel in the natural flavors of the Cucumber Tuna Avocado Salad. This power-packed salad satisfies your palate and aids in weight loss, making it a perfect high-protein meal. Indulge in its nutrient-rich goodness and make your weight loss journey a delicious experience.

Recipe 84: Avocado Shrimp Salad With Dressing

Immerse yourself in the tangy and refreshing taste of our Avocado Shrimp Salad with Dressing. Loaded with protein, it aids weight loss and offers a tasty twist to your daily diet. The simplicity of this salad makes it perfect for a healthy lunch or light dinner.

Servings: 4

Prepping Time: 15 Minutes

Cook Time: 10 Minutes

Difficulty: Easy

Ingredients:

- ✓ 1 lb large shrimp, peeled and deveined
- ✓ 2 ripe avocados, diced
- ✓ 1/2 red onion, finely chopped
- ✓ Juice of 1 large lime

- ✓ 1 tsp honey

- ✓ 3 tbsp olive oil

- ✓ 2 tbsp chopped fresh cilantro

- ✓ Salt and pepper to taste

Step-by-Step Preparation:

1. Heat 1 tbsp olive oil in a pan and cook shrimp until pink. Set aside to cool.

2. Combine lime juice, remaining olive oil, honey, salt, and pepper in a bowl for dressing.

3. Toss shrimp, avocados, and onion in a salad bowl.

4. Pour dressing over the salad and sprinkle with cilantro.

Nutritional Facts: (Per serving)

- ❖ Calories: 380

- ❖ Protein: 24g

- ❖ Carbohydrates: 15g

- ❖ Dietary Fiber: 7g

- ❖ Fat: 28g

Welcome to a world of delicious health with the Avocado Shrimp Salad with Dressing. A harmonious blend of crunchy shrimp, creamy avocado, and tangy dressing that will make your taste buds rejoice. Lose weight without losing the joy of eating with this delightful high-protein salad.

Recipe 85: Grilled Chicken Salad

Unveil a healthy yet tantalizing dish perfect for your weight loss journey: the Classic American Grilled Chicken Salad. Savor the grilled chicken atop crunchy romaine, accentuated with a melange of onions, bacon, and Parmesan, all tied together with a tangy Caesar dressing.

Servings: 4

Prepping Time: 20 minutes

Cook Time: 15 minutes

Difficulty: Easy

Ingredients:

- ✓ 4 Chicken breasts
- ✓ 2 heads of romaine lettuce
- ✓ 1 cup Caesar dressing
- ✓ 2 medium onions
- ✓ 6 slices of bacon

- ✓ 1 cup shredded Parmesan cheese
- ✓ 4 tablespoons olive oil
- ✓ Juice of 2 lemons
- ✓ Salt and pepper to taste

Step-by-Step Preparation:

1. Marinate chicken with lemon juice, olive oil, salt, and pepper. Set aside for 15 minutes.

2. Grill chicken on each side for about 7 minutes or until thoroughly cooked. Let it rest for a few minutes before slicing.

3. Chop the lettuce and onions, fry the bacon until crispy, and crumble it.

4. Combine the lettuce, onions, bacon, Parmesan, and grilled chicken slices in a large salad bowl.

5. Drizzle with Caesar dressing, toss well to combine.

Nutritional Facts: (Per serving):

- ❖ Calories: 450 kcal
- ❖ Protein: 38g
- ❖ Fat: 22g
- ❖ Carbohydrates: 15g
- ❖ Sodium: 450mg
- ❖ Fiber: 3g

Incorporate this Classic American Grilled Chicken Salad into your weight loss plan for a high-protein, flavorful feast. This salad brings a delectable mix of ingredients and a wholesome, nutritious profile to help you reach your fitness goals.

Recipe 86: Healthy Hearty Diet Salad

Embark on a journey of healthy eating with this hearty, diet-friendly salad. Packed with low-glycemic ingredients like arugula, spinach, eggs, tomatoes, and cheese vibrant dish offers a perfect balance of nutrients. Ideal for weight loss, this high-protein meal is not just beneficial but also exceptionally delicious.

Servings: 4

Prepping Time: 15 Minutes

Cook Time: 5 Minutes

Difficulty: Easy

Ingredients:

- ✓ 4 cups fresh arugula
- ✓ 4 cups fresh spinach
- ✓ 4 large boiled eggs
- ✓ 2 large tomatoes, diced
- ✓ 1 cup low-fat cheese, cubed

- ✓ 2 tbsp olive oil
- ✓ Salt and pepper to taste

Step-by-Step Preparation:

1. Rinse and dry the arugula and spinach.
2. Slice boiled eggs and dice the tomatoes.
3. Toss the greens, eggs, tomatoes, and cheese in a large bowl.
4. Drizzle olive oil, then season with salt and pepper.
5. Toss well to combine, then serve.

Nutritional Facts: (Per serving)

- ❖ Calories: 250
- ❖ Protein: 18g
- ❖ Fat: 15g
- ❖ Carbs: 10g
- ❖ Fiber: 4g
- ❖ Sugar: 3g

Reward your body with this nutrient-rich, protein-packed salad that supports weight loss. Easy to prepare and incredibly satiating, this salad with low-glycemic ingredients will keep you full for hours. So, say goodbye to unhealthy snacking and hello to a nutritious and hearty meal that's as beneficial as it is appetizing.

Recipe 87: Chickpea and Spinach Vegan Vegetable Salad

Rejuvenate your taste buds with our Chickpea and Spinach Vegan Vegetable Salad, a delightful mélange of colorful veggies, protein-packed chickpeas, and robust flavors. This nutritious salad is a perfect addition to your weight loss journey and an excellent source of plant-based protein.

Servings: 4

Prepping Time: 20 minutes

Cook Time: 10 minutes

Difficulty: Easy

Ingredients:

- ✓ 1 cup canned chickpeas, rinsed and drained
- ✓ 2 cups fresh spinach leaves
- ✓ 1 broccoli head, cut into florets
- ✓ 1 sweet red pepper, thinly sliced

- ✓ 1/2 cup black olives, pitted
- ✓ 2 zucchini, sliced and grilled
- ✓ 2 tablespoons olive oil
- ✓ Juice of 1 lemon
- ✓ Salt and pepper to taste

Step-by-Step Preparation:

1. Start by grilling zucchini slices until they get a nice char.

2. Combine the grilled zucchini, chickpeas, spinach, broccoli, sweet pepper, and olives in a large bowl.

3. Whisk together olive oil, lemon juice, salt, and pepper in a small bowl to make the dressing.

4. Pour the dressing over the salad, toss gently until all ingredients are well coated.

5. Serve immediately or refrigerate for later consumption.

Nutritional Facts: (Per serving)

- ❖ Calories: 230
- ❖ Protein: 10g
- ❖ Fat: 10g
- ❖ Carbohydrates: 30g
- ❖ Fiber: 8g
- ❖ Sodium: 180mg

Liven up your meal times with this Chickpea and Spinach Vegan Vegetable Salad. Not only is it bursting with flavors, but it also packs a protein punch. It's low in calories and fiber and perfect for weight loss. A simple recipe that brings together health, taste, and ease of preparation - a trifecta you can't resist!

Recipe 88: Quinoa Salad With Cabbage

Embark on a culinary journey that combines a nutritious blend of flavors with our high-protein Quinoa Salad recipe. This salad, made with cabbage, edamame, carrots, cucumber, red pepper, cilantro, and sesame seeds, is a delectable choice for those focusing on weight loss and seeking a hearty, protein-rich meal.

Servings: 4

Prepping Time: 20 minutes

Cook Time: 15 minutes

Difficulty: Easy

Ingredients:

- ✓ 1 cup quinoa
- ✓ 2 cups red cabbage, shredded
- ✓ 1 cup shelled edamame, cooked
- ✓ 1 cup grated carrot
- ✓ 1 cucumber, diced

- ✓ 1 red bell pepper, diced
- ✓ 1/2 cup fresh cilantro, chopped
- ✓ 2 tablespoons sesame seeds
- ✓ Salt and pepper to taste
- ✓ For the dressing: 3 tablespoons soy sauce, 1 tablespoon sesame oil, 1 tablespoon rice vinegar, 1 teaspoon honey or agave nectar

Step-by-Step Preparation:

1. Cook the quinoa according to package instructions and let it cool.
2. Combine the cooked quinoa, cabbage, edamame, carrot, cucumber, red pepper, and cilantro in a large bowl.
3. Whisk together the dressing ingredients.
4. Pour the dressing over the salad and mix well.
5. Season with salt, pepper, and sprinkle with sesame seeds before serving.

Nutritional Facts: (Per serving)

- ❖ Calories: 275 kcal
- ❖ Protein: 12 g
- ❖ Carbs: 40 g
- ❖ Fat: 8 g
- ❖ Fiber: 8 g
- ❖ Sugar: 6 g

Delight your taste buds while adhering to your weight loss goals with this protein-packed Quinoa Salad. Perfect for meal preps or a quick lunch, this colorful, texture-rich salad fills you with essential nutrients and brings an exotic twist to your regular salad routine. Eat healthy, and stay fit!

Recipe 89: Salmon Fillet Salad With Raspberry Vinaigrette

This summer, experience the flavorful fusion of pan-seared salmon fillets, fresh garden greens, and an irresistible raspberry vinaigrette. This high-protein, low-carb dish is perfect for those aiming for weight loss without sacrificing taste.

Servings: 4

Prepping Time: 15 minutes

Cook Time: 15 minutes

Difficulty: Intermediate

Ingredients:

- ✓ 4 salmon fillets
- ✓ 8 cups mixed salad greens
- ✓ 1 cup fresh raspberries
- ✓ 1/4 cup olive oil

- ✓ 2 tablespoons balsamic vinegar
- ✓ 1 tablespoon honey
- ✓ Salt and pepper to taste

Step-by-Step Preparation:

1. Sear the salmon fillets in a hot pan until fully cooked.
2. Toss the salad greens in a large bowl.
3. Blend raspberries, olive oil, vinegar, honey, salt, and pepper to make the vinaigrette.
4. Drizzle the vinaigrette over the salad.
5. Top with the seared salmon fillets.

Nutritional Facts: (Per serving)

- ❖ Calories: 310
- ❖ Protein: 32g
- ❖ Carbs: 8g
- ❖ Fat: 16g
- ❖ Fiber: 3g
- ❖ Sugar: 5g

Celebrate the season's best with this Bowl of Salmon Fillet Salad with Raspberry Vinaigrette. Packed with protein, it's a meal and a step towards your weight loss goals. Enjoy this refreshing, delectable, and nutritious salad anytime for a satisfying, guilt-free indulgence.

Recipe 90: Salad With Baked Turkey, Apple, Celery

Savor the fresh flavors of this high-protein salad featuring baked turkey, juicy apples, crisp celery, and velvety Greek yogurt. A perfect blend of texture and taste, it's a deliciously light way to nourish your body while promoting weight loss.

Servings: 4

Prepping Time: 15 minutes

Cook Time: 20 minutes

Difficulty: Easy

Ingredients:

- ✓ 500 grams of turkey breast
- ✓ 2 medium apples, cored and chopped
- ✓ 4 stalks of celery, chopped
- ✓ 4 cups of mixed green salad

- ✓ 1 cup of Greek yogurt

- ✓ 1 tablespoon of olive oil

- ✓ Salt and pepper to taste

Step-by-Step Preparation:

1. Preheat oven to 180°C/350°F. Season turkey with salt, pepper, and olive oil. Bake for 20 minutes or until fully cooked. Let it cool, and chop it into bite-sized pieces.

2. Combine chopped turkey, apples, celery, and mixed green salad in a large bowl.

3. Add Greek yogurt as a dressing and mix until all ingredients are coated evenly.

4. Season with additional salt and pepper if needed.

5. Serve immediately, or refrigerate to let the flavors meld.

Nutritional Facts: (Per serving)

- ❖ Calories: 275 kcal

- ❖ Protein: 35 grams

- ❖ Carbohydrates: 15 grams

- ❖ Fat: 8 grams

- ❖ Fiber: 3 grams

- ❖ Sugar: 10 grams

Relish this delicious, protein-packed salad with a delightful crunch from apples and celery, enveloped in a creamy Greek yogurt dressing. A meal in itself satiates your hunger and aids in weight loss while delighting your taste buds with an amalgamation of fresh, wholesome flavors.

Chapter 10: Protein-Enriched Soups

Recipe 91: Delicious Chicken and White Bean Stew

Experience the flavors of a hearty, high-protein meal with this Delicious Chicken and White Bean Stew. Packed with lean chicken and fibrous white beans provides nutrition and comfort in every spoonful, perfect for anyone seeking weight loss without compromising taste.

Servings: 6

Prepping Time: 15 minutes

Cook Time: 45 minutes

Difficulty: Medium

Ingredients:

- ✓ 2 tablespoons olive oil
- ✓ 1.5 pounds of skinless chicken breasts cut into pieces

- ✓ 1 large onion, chopped and 2 cloves garlic, minced
- ✓ 1 cup carrots, diced
- ✓ 2 cans (15 oz each) of white beans, drained and rinsed
- ✓ 4 cups chicken broth and 2 teaspoons thyme
- ✓ Salt and pepper to taste and Fresh parsley for garnish

Step-by-Step Preparation:

1. Heat oil in a large pot, add chicken pieces, and cook until browned. Remove and set aside.

2. Add onions, garlic, and carrots in the same pot, and saute until softened.

3. Return chicken to pot and add white beans, chicken broth, and thyme. Season with salt and pepper.

4. Bring to a boil, then reduce heat and simmer for 30 minutes.

5. Garnish with fresh parsley before serving.

Nutritional Facts: (Per serving)

- ❖ Calories: 380
- ❖ Protein: 42g
- ❖ Carbohydrates: 32g
- ❖ Fat: 10g
- ❖ Fiber: 8g
- ❖ Sugar: 3g

Savor the warmth of this Delicious Chicken and White Bean Stew, an essential recipe for your high-protein diet. Ideal for a cozy dinner or a post-workout meal, this dish blends nourishment and culinary delight, aiding your weight loss journey without sacrificing satisfaction. Enjoy!

Recipe 92: Golden Lentil Spinach Soup

Indulge in the hearty flavors of this Golden Lentil Spinach Soup, a delicious yet health-focused dish. This protein-packed recipe is perfect for those on a weight loss journey or seeking a wholesome meal.

Servings: 4

Prepping Time: 15 Minutes

Cook Time: 45 Minutes

Difficulty: Easy

Ingredients:

- ✓ 1 cup of dried lentils
- ✓ 1 tablespoon olive oil
- ✓ 1 onion, diced
- ✓ 2 cloves garlic, minced
- ✓ 1 teaspoon turmeric
- ✓ 1 teaspoon cumin

- ✓ 4 cups vegetable broth
- ✓ 2 cups fresh spinach
- ✓ Salt and pepper to taste

Step-by-Step Preparation:

1. Heat olive oil over medium heat, add onion and garlic and cook until softened.

2. Add turmeric and cumin, and cook for another minute.

3. Add lentils and vegetable broth, boil, then reduce heat and simmer for 30-40 minutes until lentils are tender.

4. Add spinach and cook until wilted.

5. Season with salt and pepper, and serve hot.

Nutritional Facts: (Per serving)

- ❖ Calories: 250
- ❖ Protein: 18g
- ❖ Fat: 4g
- ❖ Carbohydrates: 37g
- ❖ Fiber: 15g
- ❖ Sodium: 500mg

Embark on a healthy gastronomic adventure with this Golden Lentil Spinach Soup. Its delightful flavor, packed with high-quality protein and fiber, is a testament that delicious and nutritious can coexist. Enjoy it as a main dish or a satisfying side in your weight loss regimen.

Recipe 93: Turkey Soup

Packed with lean protein and filled with vegetables, this hearty Turkey Soup is a perfect choice for those watching their weight. An easy and satisfying meal that you can prepare, perfect for those chilly nights when you want comfort without the extra calories.

Servings: 6

Prepping Time: 20 minutes

Cook Time: 1 hour

Difficulty: Easy

Ingredients:

- ✓ 1 lb cooked turkey, shredded
- ✓ 1 medium onion, chopped
- ✓ 2 cloves garlic, minced
- ✓ 2 carrots, chopped
- ✓ 2 stalks of celery, chopped

- ✓ 1 cup frozen peas
- ✓ 6 cups low-sodium chicken broth
- ✓ 1/2 teaspoon thyme
- ✓ Salt and pepper to taste
- ✓ Chopped parsley for garnish

Step-by-Step Preparation:

1. In a large pot, sauté onion and garlic until translucent.
2. Add carrots and celery, and cook until softened.
3. Add turkey, broth, peas, and thyme. Bring to a boil.
4. Reduce heat, let it simmer for about 45 minutes.
5. Season with salt, pepper, and garnish with parsley before serving.

Nutritional Facts: (Per serving)

- ❖ Calories: 210
- ❖ Protein: 25g
- ❖ Carbohydrates: 16g
- ❖ Fiber: 3g
- ❖ Fat: 5g

This Turkey Soup doesn't just help in weight loss. It's a nourishing and warm dish that brings comfort to the table. Easily customizable, this soup is an excellent way to use leftover turkey. Savor the wholesome goodness in every spoonful, reminding you that healthy doesn't have to mean flavorless.

Recipe 94: Polish Sour Cucumber Soup With Dill

Discover the wholesome goodness of the Polish Sour Cucumber Soup with Dill. This traditional Eastern European delicacy offers a compelling blend of tangy cucumbers and fresh dill, packed with high protein to support your weight loss goals.

Servings: 4

Prepping Time: 15 minutes

Cook Time: 30 minutes

Difficulty: Easy

Ingredients:

- ✓ 4 giant sour pickles, grated
- ✓ 2 tablespoons olive oil
- ✓ 1 large onion, finely chopped
- ✓ 2 cloves of garlic, minced

- ✓ 4 cups vegetable broth
- ✓ 1 cup cooked white beans
- ✓ 2 tablespoons chopped fresh dill
- ✓ Salt and pepper to taste

Step-by-Step Preparation:

1. Heat oil in a pot, add onion and garlic and saute until translucent.

2. Add grated pickles and broth, and bring to a simmer.

3. Stir in cooked beans, and simmer for 20 minutes.

4. Season with salt, pepper, and fresh dill. Serve hot.

Nutritional Facts: (Per serving)

- ❖ Calories: 200
- ❖ Protein: 12g
- ❖ Fat: 8g
- ❖ Carbs: 25g
- ❖ Fiber: 6g

Savor the heartwarming Polish Sour Cucumber Soup with Dill, a high-protein meal for weight loss. Enjoy its vibrant flavors while reaping the benefits of its nutritional profile. This simple yet delectable soup shows that dieting doesn't mean sacrificing taste and satisfaction.

Recipe 95: Zucchini Creamy Soup

Experience a delicious twist on healthy eating with our Zucchini Creamy Soup recipe. This high-protein meal is perfect for weight loss, combining subtle flavors and nutritious ingredients to satisfy your taste buds without compromising your diet.

Servings: 4 people

Prepping Time: 15 minutes

Cook Time: 25 minutes

Difficulty: Easy

Ingredients:

- ✓ 4 medium zucchinis, cubed
- ✓ 1 large onion, diced
- ✓ 2 cloves garlic, minced
- ✓ 2 cups vegetable broth
- ✓ 1 cup skim milk

- ✓ 1 cup Greek yogurt
- ✓ 1 tablespoon olive oil
- ✓ Salt and pepper to taste

Step-by-Step Preparation:

1. Heat olive oil over medium heat, add onion and garlic, and sauté until golden.
2. Add zucchini, and cook until softened.
3. Pour in vegetable broth and simmer for 10 minutes.
4. Let it cool slightly, then blend until smooth.
5. Return the soup to the pot, add skim milk and Greek yogurt.
6. Stir well, season with salt and pepper, and simmer for 5 minutes.
7. Serve warm, and enjoy.

Nutritional Facts: (Per serving)

- ❖ Calories: 160
- ❖ Protein: 10g
- ❖ Fat: 3g
- ❖ Carbs: 24g
- ❖ Fiber: 4g

Our Zucchini Creamy Soup recipe is another healthy dish and a symphony of flavors you can enjoy without feeling guilty. It's high in protein, low in fat, and filled with zucchini goodness, making it the perfect weight-loss companion.

Recipe 96: Squash Soup With Rosemary and Paprika

Enjoy the unique combination of hearty squash, fragrant rosemary, and smoky paprika in this flavorful and high-protein Squash Soup. It's an excellent choice for those following a weight-loss regimen and wanting a filling, nutritious meal without sacrificing taste or satisfaction.

Servings: 4

Prepping Time: 15 minutes

Cook Time: 45 minutes

Difficulty: Easy

Ingredients:

- ✓ 2 medium-sized squash
- ✓ 2 tbsp olive oil
- ✓ 1 onion, diced
- ✓ 3 cloves garlic, minced

- ✓ 1 tsp dried rosemary and 1 tsp smoked paprika
- ✓ 4 cups vegetable broth
- ✓ 1 cup cooked white beans
- ✓ Salt and pepper to taste

Step-by-Step Preparation:

1. Preheat the oven to 400°F (200°C), halve the squash, and scoop out the seeds.

2. Drizzle the halves with olive oil, season with salt, and roast for 30 minutes.

3. In a large pot, sauté onion and garlic until translucent.

4. Add the cooked squash, rosemary, paprika, and broth to the pot.

5. Simmer until everything is tender, then add the white beans.

6. Use an immersion blender to puree the soup to your desired consistency.

7. Season with salt and pepper, then serve hot.

Nutritional Facts: (Per serving)

- ❖ Calories: 280
- ❖ Protein: 15g
- ❖ Carbs: 45g
- ❖ Fat: 7g
- ❖ Fiber: 9g

Experience the cozy comfort of this Squash Soup with Rosemary and Paprika. Its enticing flavors, robust nutrition profile, and satiating properties make it a perfect companion on your weight-loss journey. Enjoy it as a standalone meal, or pair it with a fresh salad for an added dose of greens.

Recipe 97: Sweet Pea, Mint Hot Soup and Dolop of Greek Yogurt

Indulge in the rich flavors and health benefits of this Sweet Pea, Mint Hot Soup topped with a dollop of Greek yogurt. This protein-packed delight not only aids in weight loss but also offers a refreshing touch to your diet, combining wholesome ingredients in a bowl.

Servings: 4

Prepping Time: 10 minutes

Cook Time: 20 minutes

Difficulty: Easy

Ingredients:

- ✓ 2 cups of fresh or frozen sweet peas
- ✓ 1 bunch of fresh mint leaves
- ✓ 2 cloves of garlic
- ✓ 1 large onion

- ✓ 1 tablespoon of olive oil

- ✓ 3 cups of vegetable broth

- ✓ Salt and pepper to taste

- ✓ 4 dollops of Greek yogurt

Step-by-Step Preparation:

1. Sauté chopped onion and garlic in olive oil until softened.

2. Add the sweet peas and broth, boil, and simmer for 15 minutes.

3. Add the mint leaves, and cook for another minute.

4. Blend the mixture until smooth, season with salt and pepper.

5. Serve hot, topped with a dollop of Greek yogurt.

Nutritional Facts: (Per serving)

- ❖ Calories: 210

- ❖ Protein: 15g

- ❖ Carbohydrates: 23g

- ❖ Fat: 6g

- ❖ Fiber: 6g

Unwind and savor the comforting blend of sweet peas, aromatic mint, and creamy Greek yogurt in this delectable soup. This high-protein meal is nourishing and helps manage weight, making it an excellent choice for health-conscious individuals seeking a hearty yet light dinner option.

Recipe 98: Hot Spicy Corn Cream Soup

Immerse yourself in the robust flavors of Hot Spicy Corn Cream Soup, adorned with crispy fried bacon and succulent shrimp. This high-protein, low-calorie delicacy is perfect for those on a weight loss journey yet unwilling to compromise on taste.

Servings: 4

Prepping Time: 15 minutes

Cook Time: 30 minutes

Difficulty: Moderate

Ingredients:

- ✓ 2 cups corn kernels
- ✓ 4 strips bacon, diced
- ✓ 200g shrimp, peeled
- ✓ 1 onion, diced and 2 cloves garlic, minced
- ✓ 1 jalapeno, seeded and minced

- ✓ 1-quart chicken broth and 1 cup heavy cream
- ✓ Salt and pepper to taste
- ✓ Fresh parsley, chopped (for garnish)

Step-by-Step Preparation:

1. In a pot, fry bacon until crispy. Remove and set aside.
2. In the same pot, sauté onions, garlic, and jalapeno.
3. Add corn, sauté until lightly browned.
4. Pour in chicken broth, and bring to a boil. Reduce heat and simmer for 20 minutes.
5. Blend the soup until smooth.
6. Return the soup to the pot, and add heavy cream, bacon, and shrimp. Cook until shrimps are pink.
7. Season with salt, pepper and garnish with parsley. Serve hot.

Nutritional Facts: (Per serving)

- ❖ Calories: 375 kcal
- ❖ Protein: 24g
- ❖ Carbohydrates: 23g
- ❖ Fat: 23g
- ❖ Fiber: 3g
- ❖ Sugar: 6g

Enrich your weight loss journey with the Hot Spicy Corn Cream Soup, blending satisfying crunches of bacon with tender shrimp bites. A symphony of bold flavors and textures in a creamy corn base, this high-protein soup promises warmth and nutritional balance in every spoonful. Enjoy!

Recipe 99: Beef and Barley Soup

Delight in the comforting, high protein Beef and Barley Soup, packed with nutritious vegetables such as carrots, tomatoes, potatoes, celery, and peas. This low-calorie dish promotes weight loss while satisfying your taste buds.

Servings: 6

Prepping Time: 20 Minutes

Cook Time: 1 Hour 30 Minutes

Difficulty: Easy

Ingredients:

- ✓ 500g lean beef, cubed
- ✓ 1 cup barley
- ✓ 2 carrots, chopped
- ✓ 1 tomato, diced
- ✓ 2 potatoes, cubed
- ✓ 2 celery sticks, chopped

- ✓ 1 cup peas
- ✓ Salt and pepper to taste
- ✓ 1 tablespoon olive oil
- ✓ 6 cups beef broth

Step-by-Step Preparation:

1. Heat the oil in a large pot over medium heat, add the beef, and brown on all sides.

2. Add the broth, barley, carrots, tomato, potatoes, celery, and peas. Season with salt and pepper.

3. Reduce heat, cover the pot, and let it simmer for about 90 minutes until the barley is tender and the flavors are well combined.

4. Adjust seasoning if necessary and serve hot.

Nutritional Facts: (Per serving)

- ❖ Calories: 300
- ❖ Protein: 30g
- ❖ Carbs: 28g
- ❖ Fiber: 6g
- ❖ Fat: 6g
- ❖ Sugar: 5g

This hearty Beef and Barley Soup delivers high-protein content and rich flavors, essential for anyone aiming for weight loss. It's a versatile meal, perfect for lunch or dinner, sure to warm you up and keep you satisfied without hindering your health goals. Enjoy this tasty, nutrient-packed bowl of goodness!

Recipe 100: Chicken Enchilada Soup

Indulge in a hearty and flavorsome Mexican-inspired dish, our Chicken Enchilada Soup. Packed with high protein ingredients, it's an ideal option for those following a weight loss regimen without compromising taste.

Servings: 6

Prepping Time: 15 minutes

Cook Time: 30 minutes

Difficulty: Easy

Ingredients:

- ✓ 2 boneless, skinless chicken breasts
- ✓ 1 large onion, chopped
- ✓ 3 cloves garlic, minced
- ✓ 1 bell pepper, chopped
- ✓ 1 can (19oz) enchilada sauce
- ✓ 4 cups chicken broth

- ✓ 1 can (15oz) black beans, drained
- ✓ 1 can (15oz) corn, drained
- ✓ 1 teaspoon cumin
- ✓ Salt and pepper to taste
- ✓ Fresh coriander for garnish

Step-by-Step Preparation:

1. In a large pot, cook the chicken breasts until done. Remove and shred.

2. In the same pot, sauté the onion, garlic, and bell pepper until softened.

3. Add the shredded chicken, enchilada sauce, broth, black beans, corn, cumin, salt, and pepper. Bring to a boil.

4. Reduce heat and simmer for about 20 minutes.

5. Serve hot, garnished with fresh coriander.

Nutritional Facts: (Per serving)

- ❖ Calories: 310
- ❖ Protein: 28g
- ❖ Fat: 8g
- ❖ Carbs: 30g
- ❖ Fiber: 8g

Enjoy this comforting bowl of Chicken Enchilada Soup, bursting with traditional flavors. It's a perfect high-protein, low-fat dish that will satisfy you and assist in your weight loss journey. Time to redefine healthy eating with this lip-smacking delight!

Conclusion

"A Visual Guide to 100 High Protein Recipes for Effective Weight Loss" by Ava Mitchell is essential to every health-conscious individual's library. This visually rich, comprehensive guide will transform your cooking, weight loss journey, and overall health.

The well-researched book provides you with protein-rich recipes that are delicious and easy to prepare and offers a comprehensive nutritional analysis of each dish. No more guesswork! You'll know what you consume regarding proteins, carbs, fats, and overall calorie count.

What's more? This guide doesn't just list recipes; it also vividly portrays them. Each dish's vibrant, high-quality images entice your culinary curiosity, inspiring you to try them out. You don't just read a recipe. You see it in all its tasty glory. The photographs ensure that you're on the right track while cooking, helping you precisely recreate the dishes.

How will this book impact your weight loss journey? (Desire) These protein-packed recipes can be the key to effective weight loss. High protein meals help curb hunger, making you feel satiated for extended periods, thus controlling overall calorie intake. Coupled with the fact that proteins have a higher thermic effect, meaning your body burns more calories digesting proteins than carbs or fats, the recipes in this guide can aid in steady and effective weight loss.

It's time to revolutionize your dietary routine. Step into the world of "A Visual Guide to 100 High Protein Recipes for Effective Weight Loss" and discover the satiating, nutritious, and delectable meals that can accelerate your weight loss journey while still delighting your taste buds. This book promises to be a game-changer in your health and fitness journey.